# Dress of the Year
## Richard Lester

Richard Lester

Foreword by Colin McDowell
Introduction by Rosemary Harden

# Dress of the Year

ACC Editions

ISBN 9781851497256

**Fashion**
Museum

British Library Cataloguing-in-Publication Data. A catalogue
record for this book is available from the British Library

Publication designed and typeset by Northbank, Bath.
northbankdesign.co.uk

Printed and bound in China

Published in England by ACC Editions, a division of the
Antique Collectors' Club Ltd., Woodbridge, Suffolk

Front cover and frontispiece
Dress of the Year 2011, by Sarah Burton for Alexander McQueen
(see also pages 186–7).

Opposite page
Raf Simons' debut show for the house of Dior included the 2012
Dress of the Year, seen here on the catwalk with *Vogue's* Anna
Wintour and Grace Coddington in the front row (see also pages
188–9). Photo: Chris Moore/Catwalking.com

# Contents

## 1971

Judith Hornby
and Blades

## 1972

Biba, Bobby
Hillson and
Orange Hand

## 1973

Christian Dior and
Yves Saint Laurent

## 1974

Missoni

## 1975

Gina Fratini and
Tommy Nutter

## 1976

Kenzo and
Fiorucci

## 1977

Kenzo

## 1978

Gordon Luke Clarke
and Cerruti

## 1979

Jean Muir

## 1980

Calvin Klein

## 1981

Karl Lagerfeld
for Chloé

## 1982

Margaret Howell
and Nigel Preston

## 1983

Sheridan Barnett

## 1984

Body Map, Betty
Jackson and
Katharine Hamnett

## 1985

Bruce Oldfield and
Scott Crolla

PAGE 102

## 1986

Giorgio Armani

PAGE 106

## 1987

John Galliano

PAGE 108

## 1988

Jean-Paul Gaultier
for Junior Gaultier

PAGE 114

## 1989

Rifat Ozbek

PAGE 116

## 1990

Romeo Gigli

PAGE 118

## 1991

Karl Lagerfeld
for Chanel

PAGE 122

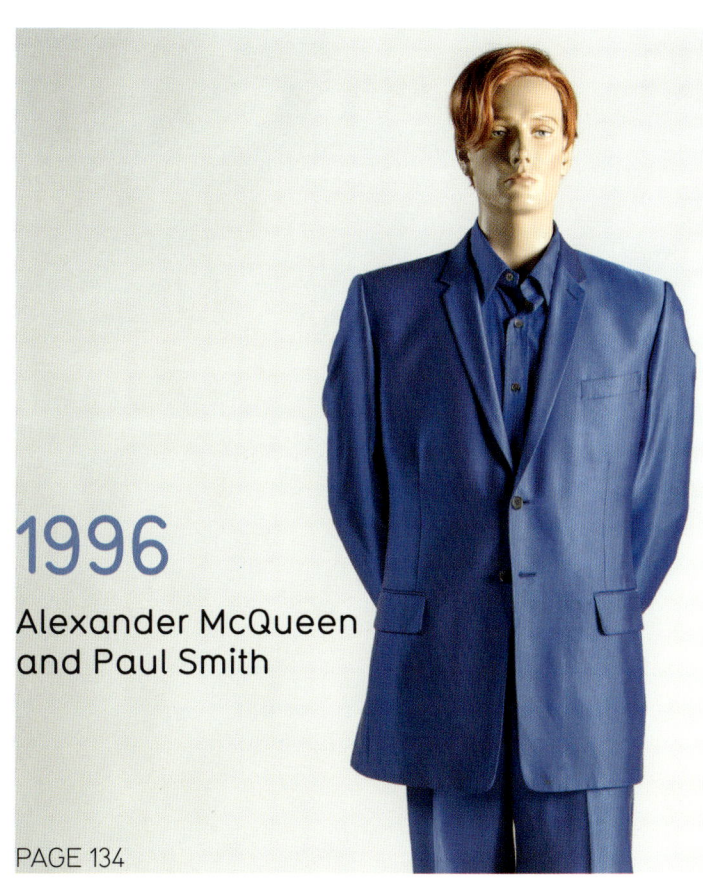

# 1999

Alexander
McQueen

# 2000

Donatella Versace
for Versace

# 2001

Tom Ford for Yves
Saint Laurent

# 2002

Junya Watanabe

# 2003

Marni

# 2004

Tom Ford for Yves
Saint Laurent

# 2005

Alber Elbaz
for Lanvin/
Thom Browne

## 2006
Prada

## 2007
Giles Deacon
for Giles

## 2008
Karl Lagerfeld
for Chanel/Kate
Moss for Topshop

## 2009
Antonio Berardi

## 2010
Dame Vivienne
Westwood

## 2011
Sarah Burton
for Alexander
McQueen

## 2012
Raf Simons for
Christian Dior

Photograph by Rei Moon

# Foreword
## Colin McDowell

In 1963 Doris Langley Moore was a power person long before the concept or expression was even invented. Her boundless enthusiasm and determination carried her along with whatever enterprise was currently obsessing her. And, as a woman perfectly used to having her own way in all things, it carried her right to the end of any campaign she embarked upon. She was a Divine Monster in the way that Peggy Guggenheim or Diana Vreeland were – women so passionate in their beliefs that they were unable to compromise. In the inhibited post-war Britain of Doris Langley Moore such people were rare, but the few – and that is certainly what they were – all had the same DNA. Often well-bred and educated, very aware of the world but keeping it at a distance, culturally omnivorous and with the determination of a tiger who has not fed her cubs for three days, women like Doris Langley Moore were formidable major players. Futhermore, they ruthlessly used their connections – they always had the right connections – to get their own way. And let us say straightaway that their failures were few. They had no time for committees of endless duration, missing the point as they argue about money and power instead of aesthetics and ensuring that the job that everyone knows has to be done is done properly. The women of whom I sing always got things done. And speedily.

And aren't we blessed that we had people like that – people who know what we need long before we know it ourselves? They are the cultural troubadours, astride their gleaming white chargers, riding forward with not a glance to left or right and unbending in their determination to achieve what they know is right and important, not just for their time but for the future. Peggy Guggenheim was perfectly aware that modern art – especially the abstraction that so disturbed her contemporaries – would eventually be understood by most of us and, some day, I am sure by all, and that is why she was a campaigner. Doris Langley Moore was even more of a visionary. When she started collecting and, more importantly, saving garments, from gloves to ball gowns, she was the only individual or organisation doing it for posterity. The Costume Collection in Manchester, founded in 1947, that predated her was the only one, which seems extraordinary when we realise how

eagerly even august museums and centres of learning now fight
for the privilege of mounting a major fashion exhibition, knowing
that it is a guaranteed money spinner. But in those days, fashion
was considered too frivolous for academics and scholars to even
consider, let alone champion as a tool for learning about ourselves
and past civilisations.

Nothing is more powerful than a hobby that develops into
a passion and from there becomes an obsession. And that was
what happened with Doris Langley Moore. Her collection grew to
such an extent that it filled her not small London house and she
felt obliged to move into a flat nearby to carry on her normal life.
Although, by then, collecting had actually become a normal and
almost everyday element of her life, Doris Langley Moore always
had wide-ranging interests, especially in the arts. She wrote books
not only on fashion but on social behaviour and history. She was a
Byron scholar and produced several books on this most complex,
albeit charismatic 19th-century character, including a seminal work
*Lord Byron: Accounts Rendered,* published to high critical acclaim
in 1974, by which time she had found a permanent home for her
collection in Bath.

Doing so was the result of a triumph of determination over
official indifference. Redoubtable, robust and when necessary
prepared to be ruthless, Doris Langley Moore was not always nice,
but people on a mission with only limited time to spare can rarely
afford the time for too many niceties. And it was a mission. Nothing
less than to make people who had never really thought of fashion
and costume as having some cultural value for contemporaries
and the future realise that it probably had more value than many
other disciplines more highly thought of at the time, disciplines that
have faded as fashion has shone. Fashion, which is cyclical, never
fails. It is the most completely renewable minor art created by man.
And it is renewable because fashion is social and its appreciation
and rejection (think of poor Amelia Bloomer and how she was
treated in the 1850s over her totally rational suggestion for a cycling
costume) is integral to daily life in ways that higher arts not always
are. It is, in fact, the art that we can all enjoy and usually

understand – although that might take some time.

And that is how Doris Langley Moore was so prescient. She knew that the way to elongate the life of most artefacts is to cosset them, love them, collect them and then share your passion by displaying them. Once she realised that her collection of clothing for men, women and children going back to the 17th century was in fact a Collection, she left no stone unturned, no avenue unexplored and no high-ranking individual with influence unlobbied in her determination to find her clothes a home other than her own house. And this is where the character of this amazing woman becomes apparent.

So, who was the woman we must thank for the collection that finally came to rest in Bath – surely the most appropriate of cities for anything to do with elegance, sophistication and style to call home?

Doris Langley Moore was born in Lancashire in 1902 but brought up and educated in South Africa where her father was a newspaper editor. But she came back to England because it was English culture and history that moved her. As a young woman, her strong features were, to use the terminology of the time, considered handsome rather than pretty. Her prominent jawline – not unlike that of the other daughter of Lancashire, Gracie Fields, who was making her own determinations known in the field of popular music – promised great things in the future. Doris went into print early with an amusing book about The Bright Young Things and the pitfalls their innocence presented for them. It was strongly tongue-in-cheek and was favourably reviewed by no less a critic and sharp observer of human frailty than Dorothy Parker who commented in *The New Yorker,* 'if only this book had been placed in my hands years ago, maybe I could have been successful instead of just successive.'

During World War II Doris Langley Moore broadened her cultural horizons by providing the scenario of a ballet, *The Quest,* choreographed by Frederick Ashton. The music was by William Walton, close friend of the Sitwells, and John Piper designed the sets and costumes. The ballet was based on Spenser's *The Faerie*

*Queene* and was danced by Moira Shearer, Margot Fonteyn, Beryl Grey and Robert Helpmann. These names alone give us a very good clue about the sort of circles Doris Langley Moore moved in. When, in 1949, her book *Women in Fashion* was published, the photographs illustrating the clothes were all posed by top actress friends such as Vivien Leigh, Vanessa Redgrave and the famous singer Elisabeth Schwarzkopf. So when, after being shown in various places, the collection finally came to Bath, it came trailing clouds of media glory – and that was one of the reasons for its instant success with the people of the city and tourists alike.

But it was the Dress of the Year, initiated in 1963, that was the most original and exciting thing of all because it took into account a new profession in the fashion world: that of the professional fashion journalist who was an expert in her (or, indeed his) field. Previously, newspaper editors thought that fashion could be lumped together with cookery, flower arrangement and knitting as subjects that any female journalists could write about. But, by the time Swinging London was born, the role of a fashion journalist was as specialist and precisely focussed as that of a theatre, art or music critic, a position it still holds today. So, what better way to keep the collection alive than by asking the specialist fashion writers to curate the accession of one new garment per year to reflect the mood of fashion and perhaps presage the next move. It also had the great advantage that all museums long for in that it provided new accessions at little or no cost to the museum in that the chosen designer is always asked to donate the garment – or in some cases garments – and none has ever refused.

So, over the years, Bath has been able to procure a collection of garments that reflect their time through the taste of one professional's individual taste and it is impressive how many of the choices have stood the test of time, and, even when they don't, those of us with long memories have to admit that the choice was right at the moment it was made. For the first three years the judges were a now-forgotten group called The Fashion Writers' Association but the long run of individual choices was initiated in 1966 by the doyenne of British fashion journalists, Ernestine Carter, the fashion editor of *The Sunday Times,* a visionary and trailblazer. She chose a now defunct label, Young Jaeger designed by Michèle Rosier of V de V for Young Jaeger. The next year was the turn of Felicity Green of the *Daily Mirror* who again chose a high street brand, Slimma by David Bond. Jean Muir was the choice of Ailsa Garland; Yves Saint Laurent was chosen by Alison Adburgham ... Margaret Howell and Nigel Preston by Grace Coddington ... Suzy Menkes went for Bruce Oldfield ... in 2002 Junya Watanabe was the choice of Hilary Alexander ... Isabella Blow selected seven designers: Hussein Chalayan, Julien Macdonald, Lainey Keogh and Deborah Milner ... and so on over the years to the most recent choices: Prada, Lagerfeld for Chanel and Antonio Berardi.

What do these choices tell us? Firstly, how remarkably forward-looking the people making the choices were, by and large. Also, how well many of the designs have stood up to changing tastes and, finally, how the clothes on display are not just clothes but also a broad history of how fashionable people were dressed over the years. Perhaps most importantly of all, one can look at these garments and find all the battles won by women in the last fifty years. And this social commentary is the importance of this very special collection. The Fashion Museum of Bath presents us with living history – and it is still very much alive and kicking today, I am pleased to say.

Colin McDowell, fashion writer and selector
of the Dress of the Year 1986

# Introduction
## Rosemary Harden

'It has been the practice of the Museum of Costume to add up-to-date specimens year by year, each one typifying a design, textile, colour, and structure likely to retain interest in the future and to be exhibited again in time to come.'

Doris Langley Moore, *Bath Assembly Rooms and The Museum of Costume, An Illustrated Souvenir*, 1964

The Fashion Museum in Bath is one of the world's great museum collections of historic and fashionable dress, and has been Designated by Arts Council England as one of outstanding national significance. The Museum includes many treasures (from exquisite Elizabethan embroidery to grand Georgian court dresses), but one of the highlights of the collection is a group of ensembles from 1963 to the present day known as the Dress of the Year collection, which represents an outstanding year-by-year record of contemporary fashion through the work of leading British, French, Italian, American and Japanese fashion designers.

The Fashion Museum came to the 18th-century Assembly Rooms in the city of Bath as the Museum of Costume in 1963, when visionary and pioneering costume collector Doris Langley Moore donated her collection of historic dress to Bath City Council. (The museum is now owned and managed by Bath and North East Somerset Council.) Mrs Langley Moore felt strongly that the museum displays should always finish with an ensemble from the current year and, with this in mind, dreamed up the Dress of the Year scheme. It remains one of the most famous of all contemporary collecting schemes within museums world-wide, and one which is the envy of our museum colleagues.

Fashion is all about the new, about change; and a museum that collects and presents objects to show developments in fashionable dress must have the machinery to regularly and systematically update the contemporary collection. The Fashion

Museum has the Dress of the Year scheme, which works like this: each year since 1963 the museum has asked a leading fashion expert to choose a dress or outfit to represent the newest and most influential ideas in contemporary fashion. The selection is donated to the museum by the designer or maker. All choice is subjective, but part of the genius of the Dress of the Year scheme is that it removes the choice from the curator, instead relying on the expertise of an industry insider to make an informed – albeit personal – selection. The selector therefore becomes as important as the selected.

Since first it started the Dress of the Year scheme has relied upon the generosity and talent of many people, and the Fashion Museum is grateful to each and every one for their insight and unswerving support – past, present and future. The list of the Dress of the Year selectors reads like a Who's Who of the great fashion editors of the past fifty years, and we are honoured that two of the selectors, Colin McDowell (1986) and Iain R Webb (1998), have generously added their expertise and support to this book. The Dress of the Year designers are the history of fashion since the 1960s, and the Fashion Museum is honoured that these stellar names have unfailingly supported the scheme since its outset, through the gift of all of the pieces selected to become part of the permanent collection at the Fashion Museum. An integral part of the scheme has also been the mannequin on which the chosen outfit was displayed in the Museum galleries: since 1963 Adel Rootstein Display Mannequins have each year very kindly donated a figure, expertly coiffured and made-up to achieve the right fashion look to go with the ensemble selected.

In 1984, Brenda Polan chose a man's oversized slogan T-shirt designed by Katharine Hamnett as Dress of the Year, and wrote 'This is the year when menswear crawled out of its fusty closet and began to dance in the streets'. In 2014, at a distance now of 30 years, this comment seems right on the button for the time, summing up how the selection marked a moment in history. Thus Ms Polan's phrase neatly and succinctly shows the importance of the Dress of the Year scheme not only to the Fashion Museum, but also to the study of fashion history in general.

In this new and authoritative book by long-time Fashion Museum supporters Richard Lester and the team at the Antique Collectors' Club, I am delighted that for the first time the whole collection – fifty years' worth of Dress of the Year selections – will be presented with informative text and striking photographs so that it can be shared widely with everyone who wants to learn more, or who is just fascinated and intrigued by the styles of the past and the development of fashion in the last half century. All of the Dress of the Year ensembles remain as part of the collection of the Fashion Museum in Bath, a publicly owned museum, and are available for everyone to see.

Rosemary Harden, Curator, Fashion Museum, Bath

# Dress of

the Year

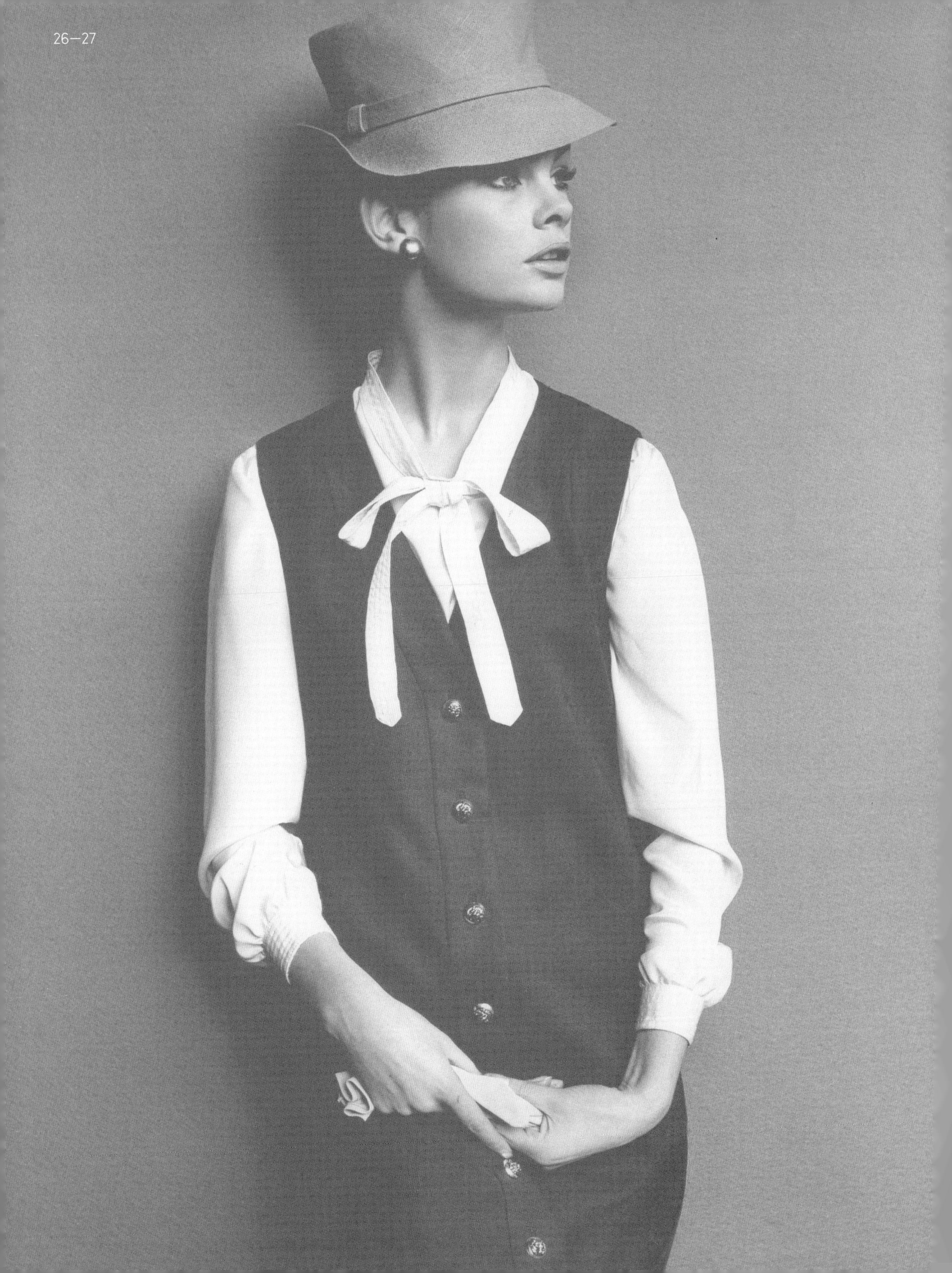

# Mary Quant

Grey wool day dress with cream chiffon blouse, hat by Reed Crawford, boots by Anello and Davide

Chosen by the Fashion Writers' Association

In 1963 British fashion had yet to experience the revolutionary changes that were to occur over the remainder of the decade, which makes the first Dress of the Year all the more important. As the first panel of selectors, The Fashion Writers' Association came from a distinguished group of established newspaper and magazine editors which included influential names such as Ernestine Carter of *The Sunday Times*.

Their choice might be said to mark the end of one style of dressing and the beginning of another, for this was still the elegant, demure early 1960s – before the mini-skirt arrived in late 1964. Mary Quant's grey wool day dress and chiffon blouse were typical of the clothes being sold from her hugely successful boutique, Bazaar, on London's King's Road, which had rapidly gained a reputation for selling trend-setting clothes for a younger clientele.

With a hem still firmly below the knee, this vaguely 1920s-inspired button-through shift dress formed the basis of a variety of looks offering customers a youthful alternative. At the time, only a small number of designers catered specifically for women in their twenties who wanted clothes to reflect the rapidly changing world in which they lived. Mary Quant's talent was to gradually incorporate the changes her boutique customers requested. Bazaar was one of the first owner/designer boutiques before the rush to the King's Road began, and its clients were independent, style-conscious and relatively wealthy (the dress cost a shade over 13 guineas, equivalent to approx. £200 today) compared to the younger trendsetters who drove the popular image of 'Swinging London' later in the decade. John French's stylish image was commissioned for *The Sunday Times* and emphasises a casual elegance that was still very much the accepted ideal of female beauty in mainstream fashion circles, with white gloves as a standard accessory; a world away from the look about to be epitomised by Twiggy and Penelope Tree.

Reed Crawford's bold, trilby-inspired hat balances Anello and Davide's stiletto boots, which hint at something a little more glamorous. Both firms were staples of the fashion scene in the 1960s; designers relied on their ever-changing styles to accessorise and (in some cases) inspire their creations.

In her autobiography, *Tongue in Chic*, Ernestine Carter said of the designer: 'It is given to a fortunate few to be born at the right time, in the right place, with the right talents. In recent fashion there are three: Chanel, Dior, and Mary Quant.'

Opposite page
Jean Shrimpton wears the first Dress of the Year by Mary Quant, photographed for *The Sunday Times* by John French.
Fashion Museum / John French

'The look of 1963. The shift dress. Slim, seamed but barely touching the body. This is typical of the young look and the great influence that the young have brought to bear.'

Fashion Writers' Association Jury

Mary Quant's original pen and ink sketches for the chosen Dress of the Year reflect the simple, elegant lines of her clothes.

Opposite page
High fashion from Mary Quant's boutique 'Bazaar' was not inexpensive: the original retail prices for the 1963 ensemble.

# MARY QUANT

Telephone: KENsington 5037
Sales: KNIghtsbridge 8477

Miss Goldsmith
Museum of Costume
City of Bath. Spa Department
Assembly Rooms Bath.                                    May 2nd 1963

Dear Miss Goldsmith,

Thank you for your letter of 1st May 1063.

I am so glad that our model in the Museum is a success.
The prices of each garment are as follows:-
Blouse 11gns
Dress 13½gns
Hat 8½gns
Boots 9½gns.

Yours sincerely

*Caroline Fairhurst*

for MARY QUANT LIMITED.

# 1964

## Jean Muir

Printed Liberty silk dress for Jane & Jane, shoes
by Christian Dior at Charles Jourdan

Chosen by the Fashion Writers' Association

'Standards should run through life and clothes are a three-dimensional way of presenting standards – standards of taste, of quality, of discipline, of integrity.'

Jean Muir interviewed by the *Financial Times*, 1991

In a career which began in the stockrooms of a department store, Jean Muir went on to develop an internationally recognised fashion brand, with her clothes chosen as Dress of the Year in 1964, 1968 and 1979; to date, the most awards of any designer selected in the scheme.

As a former employee of Liberty, Jean Muir's early career was surrounded by just the kind of distinctive floral print she selected for her winning design in 1964, in a shape which was to pervade the entire decade: the elegant empire line.

After a six-year stint with Jaeger she began designing for Jane & Jane in 1962, and like fellow award recipients Mary Quant and John Bates, who also founded careers in the London ready-to-wear market in the late 1950s, she shared a desire to inject new life into clothes for younger clients.

With Jane & Jane she had yet to develop the hallmark style with which she was later identified. The 1964 Dress of the Year owes much to the established code of formal dressing in the immediate post-war period, but the vibrant Liberty print silk gives just a hint of the change about to erupt on to the British fashion scene.

In her use of quality fabrics and prints her aim was to raise the general standard of ready-to-wear, bringing a little of the quality associated with couture into the process. Paired with shoes by Christian Dior at Charles Jourdan, this was by no means an inexpensive ensemble, but it was still a shade more affordable than the 40 guineas needed to purchase Mary Quant's 1963 creation complete from Bazaar.

It was not until she opened her own label in 1966 that Jean Muir's true colours began to be seen, and for much of her career these were navy and black – perennial favourites for her definitive jersey and crêpe dresses.

'This is meant to be worn extremely short – three inches above the knee.'

Doris Langley Moore

# John Bates

'Casbah' dress for Jean Varon in printed linen with netting midriff, shoes by Anello and Davide

Chosen by the Fashion Writers' Association

With the exotic name 'Casbah', John Bates' 1965 mini dress for Jean Varon was a dress that launched a thousand copies. Riding high on the rapid success of his ready-to-wear firm Jean Varon, he was championed by progressive fashion editors such as Marit Allen at *Vogue*. Finally, he was receiving credit for ground-breaking uses of space-age fabrics, revealing and concealing panels, and – as his original sketch for the dress confirms – the 'total look' specifying make-up, shoes and hair.

John Bates' fashionable clients wanted shorter hems and shorter hair; the new ideal was to be what the *Daily Express* referred to that year as the Jean Varon 'little girl look'. 'Casbah' was photographed on Jean Shrimpton, this time by Brian Duffy for *Vogue*. The contrast with John French's image of her wearing the 1963 Dress of the Year is noteworthy, not only for the chameleon-like quality of the model but also for the increasingly revealing nature of the clothes.

The Jean Varon ideal revealed in John Bates' original sketch of the ensemble is recognisable as the typical 1960s girl; Twiggy as compared to Barbara Goalen. But no designer can guarantee the way in which their designs are photographed by the fashion press once outside their influence. *Honey* magazine saw their ideal girl as ringleted and sweet when they photographed the dress in June 1965, and designers and editors alike often bemoaned the way the new shorter fashions were portrayed, the ultimate sin being the wearing of high heels with the mini dress.

Anello and Davide's answer was low, almost flat-heeled pumps that increased the feeling of youth and innocence, as specified by John Bates in his design. Founded in the West End in 1922, their clients included everyone from the Beatles to the major fashion houses, with their shop on Drury Lane being well established as a stop-off for designers and the fashionable on the early London boutique scene.

Opposite page
**Jean Shrimpton injected a sophisticated sex appeal to the mini dress, photographed by Brian Duffy.**
Fashion Museum/Brian Duffy

*jean*
# VARON
*couture et prêt à porter*

Spa Director,
City of Bath Spa Dept.,
Assembley Rooms,
Bath.

20th July, 1965.

Dea r Sirs,

We wish to thank you for your letter of 15th
July with reference to our dress style "Casbah".
This dress retailed at 6gns and sold in a fantastic
quantity we in fact completely sold out of the original
print and customers were forced to accept orders in
several other fabrics and colours.

We enclose herwith the required sketch for
your make-up depa rtment.

Yours faithfully,

Susan Jarrett.
Showroom Manageress.

**JEAN VARON LTD.**    **17 WOODSTOCK STREET, LONDON, W.1**    *Mayfair 2233*

DIRECTORS :    *B. L. BRAGG*    *E. B. WEST*    *J. E. BATES*

Opposite page
'Casbah' was a runaway success and
sold out in several designways, helping
to propel John Bates and his company
Jean Varon into the public eye.

The whole lid black.
False eyelashes (Triple thickness), heavily mascareno but straight — not curly.
Palest pink (almost white with a pink tinge.)

Hair Vidal Sasoon.

nail varnish very silver pink. again almost white.

navy blue.

Shoes   Arnello + Davide.

Opposite page
*Honey* magazine photographed the dress in June 1965, preferring their model to show the 'little girl' look which chimed with rapidly rising hemlines and simple shift silhouettes.
Honey/IPC Magazines. From the archive of Liz Eggleston: vintage-a-peel.co.uk

# 1966

# Michèle Rosier, Young Jaeger and Simone Mirman

Clear PVC coat with banded decoration by Michèle Rosier of V de V, black and white linen dress by Young Jaeger, visor hat by Simone Mirman, boots by Elliot, tights by John Bates for Echo

Chosen by Ernestine Carter at *The Sunday Times*

Ernestine Carter had not always been a fan of the innovations brought about by the likes of Michèle Rosier and it was often down to the younger fashion writers under her editorship at *The Sunday Times* to convince her which fashion star was in the ascendant. This system was to pay dividends, however, and together with her columnists Brigid Keenan and Caroline Coulthurst, she lent her considerable influence to support designers such as John Bates, Jean Muir and Michèle Rosier.

Her choice for 1966 is as extraordinary as it is bold, for it breaks with the past almost completely to provide a vision of space-age glamour in modern plastics. In the palette of Mondrian made famous by Yves Saint Laurent a year earlier, and with just three years to go before man took his first steps on the moon, Michèle Rosier proffered her version of the space race early; along with John Bates and Mary Quant, she specialised in short, sharp and challenging clothes.

By 1966 the mini-skirt had arrived on the British fashion scene and was not to disappear from the fashion pages until the mid-1970s. Jaeger, like many other respected British ready-to-wear houses, had launched 'Young Jaeger' to compete in a market which saw increased spending power from clients in their twenties and thirties, a group that had previously emulated their parents' tastes in clothes. London's fashion houses were by now producing ready-to-wear lines. The London branches of Christian Dior had 'Diorling', Frederick Starke chose 'Frederica', and Austin Reed produced 'Cue'. Just as today, they produced high fashion 'mix and match' elements. These were seldom worn as a total ensemble, as styled for the Dress of the Year, but more usually sold separately and integrated into practical wardrobes.

Simone Mirman's visor hat in tinted PVC is a remarkable feat, given that it was designed by a milliner more famous for her creations for the British Royal family throughout the 1960s and 1970s. Despite being a pillar of the established millinery trade, her early years were spent designing for Elsa Schiaparelli's London branch, channelling her evident sense of fun into producing designs for one of the 20th century's most influential designers. In her mid-fifties when the 1966 Dress of the Year was chosen, she and Ernestine Carter proved that it was not just London's youngest designers who were willing to embrace change.

Opposite page
The Dress of the Year award was supported by legendary fashion writer Ernestine Carter, who photographed her choice for *The Sunday Times* in 1966.

'This is the year of the see-through. From the PVC visored hat to the PVC boots, the look is transparent. This is the year that plastics became not only of fashion age, but the fashion rage.'

Ernestine Carter

# 1967

## David Bond for Slimma

Woman's trouser suit for Slimma, hat by Edward Mann, shoes by Saxone

Chosen by Felicity Green at the *Daily Mirror*

Until the late 1960s there were some things in the fashion world that were just not done. One was to wear a trouser suit to dinner or to the races, and in a series of stunts a number of fashion writers had publically challenged the rules for their editorials, with varying results. By 1967 things were beginning to change and the burgeoning ready-to-wear market was one of Britain's greatest success stories. There was no better example than Slimma. Founded in 1935, the brand name purportedly derived from the phrase 'Slim-mothers'; the firm was immensely successful in the middle market, particularly noted for just the kind of vibrant trouser suits chosen by Felicity Green for Dress of the Year.

David Bond designed under the 'Slimma Group One' label and produced what he called the 'Total Look', as advertised by Twiggy in the fashion pages. Slimma coordinated a new, brighter palette of oranges and pinks into tightly tailored jackets, pencil trousers (many in the newly available elasticated fabrics) and versions of the ever popular ski-pants. Felicity Green knew readers of the *Daily Mirror* did not have limitless funds to spend on fashion, so her choice for 1967 was very much the brand of bright and new fashion available country-wide via quality department stores.

Also sweeping the country in the second half of the decade was *Avengers* fever: what Diana Rigg wore on the new television show in the character of Emma Peel, so the people wanted. Edward Mann provided many of her hats in the series, and was for a brief period London's milliner of choice, renowned for his wide-brimmed felt styles personified by the classic fedora. Models Pattie Boyd and Celia Hammond were famously photographed by John French wearing Mann's avant garde space-age styles in 1965. By 1967 he was looking to a nostalgic bohemian past, the world of Oscar Wilde, Art Nouveau and swirling cloaks that inspired the one-off style made especially for this Dress of the Year ensemble.

Originally a Scottish manufacturer of quality, by the late 1960s Saxone was among many brands acquired by the British Shoe Corporation. It was one of several high street names with which Felicity Green's readers would have been familiar, along with the likes of Dolcis, Freeman Hardy & Willis, and Lilley & Skinner. All produced fashionable, affordable copies of more expensive styles, looking to names like The Chelsea Cobbler or Anello and Davide to provide inspiration for their high fashion ranges.

The *Daily Mirror* features the 1967 Dress of the Year as the award becomes an annual event for the fashion columns of Fleet Street.

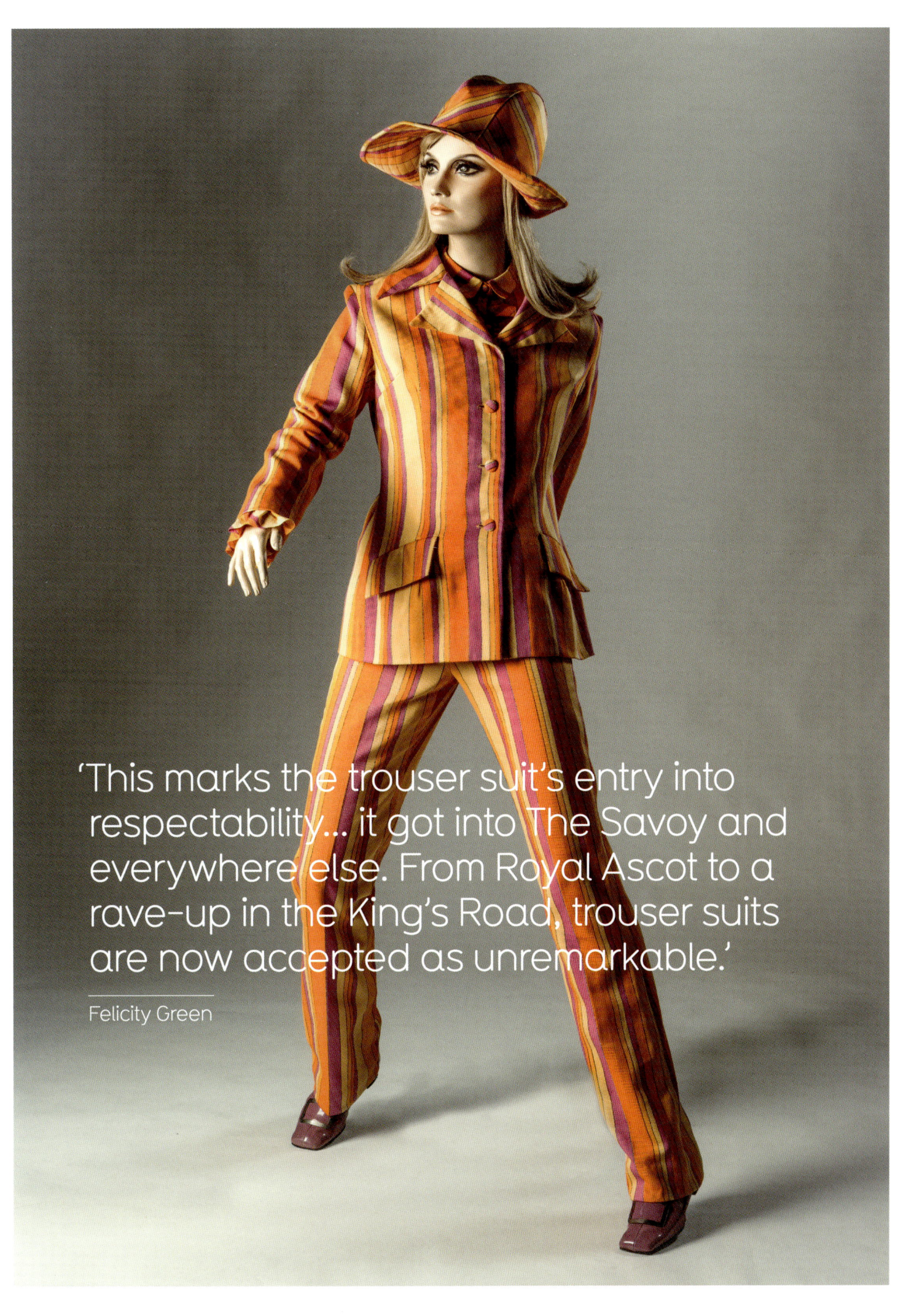

'This marks the trouser suit's entry into respectability... it got into The Savoy and everywhere else. From Royal Ascot to a rave-up in the King's Road, trouser suits are now accepted as unremarkable.'

Felicity Green

# Jean Muir

Black and white spotted cotton voile dress by Jean Muir, shoes by Bally

Chosen by Ailsa Garland at *Fashion* magazine
Rootstein Sandie Shaw mannequin

As the 1960s drew to a close it was up to Jean Muir to define the new feminine ideal with an empire line dress which could not be more of a contrast to the futuristic visions of some designers just a few years before. Gone were the PVCs, sky-high hems and forward-looking styling, to be replaced by a historically inspired vision of frills and femininity, owing more to Jane Austen than the space race.

As editor of British *Vogue* between 1961 and 1964, Ailsa Garland had been a well-placed fashion observer. Her steely intuition had famously led to her using David Bailey's New York shots of Jean Shrimpton in *Vogue* against her superior's wishes. At the newly opened *Fashion* magazine she now applied the same instincts to finding the next big thing, this time aimed at her younger but nonetheless affluent readership.

The empire line of Jean Muir's pretty summer dress was perhaps the most influential shape of the late 1960s and early 1970s, the new longer length immediately adopted for day and evening wear; but in contrast to its early 1960s incarnation, this time it was regularly used with bold prints on the new synthetic fabrics like Tricel. The shape is essentially historical, grounded in the early 19th century, but whereas the early 1960s version would usually be in a stiff slub silk or satin, the late 1960s incarnation adds full sleeves, and a fluidity accentuated by the use of cotton voile in the 1968 Dress of the Year.

Other exponents of the romantic revival over subsequent years included Laura Ashley, who excelled in a similar way, using a substantial archive of printed cotton designs and producing a vast array of goods from factories in Carno, Wales. Gina Fratini layered lace and petticoats to create a new vision of Victorian dress; like Jean Muir, her dresses were expensive and widely copied. Interestingly, this look is not one for which Jean Muir is best remembered, and by the early 1970s she had adopted a much plainer style, rapidly establishing as her hallmark the unparalleled use of overstitched moss crêpe and jersey.

Swiss firm Bally's shoes were, and still are, the height of mainstream luxury, and the low black patent pumps reaffirm the romantic appeal of the 1968 Dress of the Year, then retailing at around £4. This style proved immensely successful throughout the 1960s, largely because of its adaptability, being suited to short and long hems, and even trouser suits.

'This is the prettiest maxi dress I've seen so far and brings out the new stories of this year; a return to more design and a feeling of romance and femininity. The squares of brilliant cloth in mini length are now out.'

Ailsa Garland

# 1969

## Ossie Clark for Quorum

Chiffon and satin trouser suit for Quorum with print by Celia Birtwell, shoes by Rayne

Chosen by Prudence Glynn at *The Times*

'This outfit exemplifies the 1969 look at its most appealing and its most subtle. This is the year of the pant dress, the year of see-through. Women's trousers should not make them look like men. See-through should never be crude enough to subtract rather than add to the promise.'

Prudence Glynn

Ossie Clark photographed in 1969 with a similar design to his Dress of the Year, combining print by Celia Birtwell with the new culotte suit.
Getty Images

Husband and wife team Ossie Clark and Celia Birtwell were the perfect late 1960s couple: glamorous and creative, friends to artists, models and singers.

Quorum was the brainchild of Alice Pollock, who also designed for her fashionable boutique located on London's King's Road. By the late 1960s the brand had, however, got into financial difficulties. Salvation came in the form of Al Radley, a ready-to-wear manufacturer who backed Quorum's wild fashion shows and glamorous premises, eventually employing other designers under the label such as Betty Jackson and Sheridan Barnett.

This was Ossie Clark at the height of his powers, designing his sought-after, sensuous clothes whilst Celia Birtwell provided innovative prints that managed to combine a nostalgia for Art Deco with a firm anchor in the present. Prudence Glynn was an enormous fan, and her choice for 1969 illustrated their talents to perfection.

Essentially a romantic vision, this Dress of the Year is also injected with a little rock star glamour: layered and concealing and yet, because of an inherent understanding of how the fabric would behave in motion, still appealing.

Under the 'Ossie Clark for Radley' label his dresses became available to a far greater audience, and this mid-priced range was hugely successful. As with this Dress of the Year, he used Celia Birtwell's prints, but this time on moss crêpes and cottons, with ribbon-edged trouser suits, daring low-cut halter neck dresses and 1930s-inspired sleek tailoring.

Used to providing shoes for another sort of fashion royalty, H & M Rayne boasted three Royal Warrants, with Sir Edward Rayne at the helm from the age of 29. Their excellence was quality, luxury and style. From a showroom on New Bond Street they made shoes for London high society and, via licensing agreements with department stores Bergdorf Goodman and Bonwit Teller, managed to conquer the all-important American market.

# Bill Gibb

Plaid wool skirt and cotton blouse by
Bill Gibb, waistcoat by Kaffe Fassett,
boots by The Chelsea Cobbler

Chosen by Beatrix Miller at *Vogue*

Bill Gibb's vision was unique, and one of the most important influences on British fashion during the late 1960s and early 1970s. His talents lay in the combination of craft, fantasy and couture standards of manufacture, all of which combined to create startling and beautiful clothes. His look was a complete one and, often employing his favourite emblem of the bee, he created layered knitted clothes of exquisite complexity and colour, delicately embroidered silks, and luxuriously fashioned leathers and furs. A hallmark was the combination of bold prints and textures, seemingly mismatched but successful because of their vibrancy. In the London of the early 1970s, only he, Thea Porter, Jean Muir and later John Bates represented the new face of British couture on the world stage.

Beatrix Miller was the much-respected editor of *Vogue* when she chose his voluminous plaid wool skirt and blouse as Dress of the Year for 1970, teamed with a knitted waistcoat by American-born designer Kaffe Fassett. As if to underline the beginning of a new decade, the break with the modish fashion of the 1960s was complete. This use of metres of bold fabric with a hint of historical grandeur was to filter down to a million maxi dresses sold by department stores, boutiques and wholesalers across the country.

From the Bill Gibb room in Harrods and his own boutique on Bond Street, he dressed stars of stage and screen, famously designing a renaissance-inspired gown that Twiggy wore to the première of *The Boyfriend* in 1971, as well as singer Lulu's wedding dress for her marriage to celebrity hairdresser John Frieda in 1977. His collaborations included Kaffe Fassett and Missoni, but he was also willing to work in the middle market, designing an exclusive range of knitted separates for the readers of *Homes and Gardens* magazine.

The 1970 Dress of the Year was also photographed by *The Sunday Times,* and the difference in styling is notable. Bill Gibb's vision is perhaps best reflected in the original shoot for the Fashion Museum; the newspaper's model was depicted as a demure hostess and so, in a story often repeated, the designer saw their creations watered down for specific newspaper and magazine readerships.

'Bill Gibb captures the essence of change with his blending of pattern, print and texture. The folkloric feeling is strong, fabrics used have deep associations; tartan and Fair Isle and the long sweeping pleats and laced sleeveless waistcoat have early origins.'

Beatrix Miller

Opposite page
As the Dress of the Year Award entered its second decade, Bill Gibb's original sketch with fabric swatches illustrated his new concept of luxury fashion, with layers of traditionally crafted textiles and knitwear.
Victoria and Albert Museum, London

In Vogue —
1970
and Sunday
Times

SHIRT SAME AS
956 .

inset √5"
√5"

86

#8

# 1971

## Judith Hornby and Blades

Hot pants suit in Liberty printed cotton by Graziella Fontana at Judith Hornby, sandals by Ravel. Gentleman's black velvet evening suit by Rupert Lycett Green at Blades

Chosen by Serena Sutcliffe at *The Daily Telegraph* and the Earl of Lichfield

For the first time, 1971 saw the Dress of the Year award expanded to include both male and female ensembles.

Judith Hornby began life as a model and moved into fashion quite by chance, initially employing a small number of freelance designers to create samples. Among them was Graziella Fontana, a designer with an impeccable CV that included working with Karl Lagerfeld at Chloé for over a decade. She combined two favourite themes of the early 1970s in one outfit, using a distinctive print from Liberty and hot pants (the shortest of shorts) whose introduction has widely been credited to Mary Quant. Judith Hornby loved combining prints, but sadly export regulations meant that her tenure at the forefront of British fashion was a short one, and as early as 1975 she was living and working in the US. By the end of the decade she was selling to over 40 stores country-wide with *The Miami News* reporting in 1979: 'She has a flair for combining unlikely patterns in multiple colour schemes and pulling off a finished not haphazard look.'

Rupert Lycett Green, by contrast, had become an established and enormously influential force in British menswear since founding Blades in the early 1960s. He had rapidly gained a reputation for beautifully cut, understated tailoring at a time when men's fashions had undergone enormous change, with the introduction of colour and (particularly in the case of Blades) luxurious velvet, damasks and silks. His only real competition came from the likes of Michael Fish (of Mr Fish) and Tommy Nutter. Both subverted traditional tailoring to produce clothes suited for the 'Piccadilly Peacocks' that populated the West End and the King's Road during the late 1960s and early 1970s – modern versions of the Regency dandy.

Operating from a Georgian town house in Mayfair, decorated to perfection by David Mlinaric, Blades offered its customers discreet luxury. Just as with women's fashions of the period, the Blades style draws on historical inspiration, this time the smoking jackets of the Edwardian era, to create a modern luxury look for men.

Chosen by the Earl of Lichfield, himself a Blades customer, it was not until Fiorucci and Kenzo appeared on the scene that this style of dress was superseded by more contemporary tailoring, particularly influenced by American and Italian ready-to-wear.

Opposite page
Patrick Lichfield was renowned as both a photographer and a modern dandy, making him a perfect choice to select one of the two outfits in 1971.
Getty Images

'Fashion is moving out of fancy dress
into the sportive, so the dress of the
year has to be a shorts outfit.'
———————————
Serena Sutcliffe

'I wanted to combine classical elegance with modern design. Although the outfit looks new and dressy today, I feel that I would not be found out of place should I have to wear it in, say, thirty years.'

Patrick Lichfield

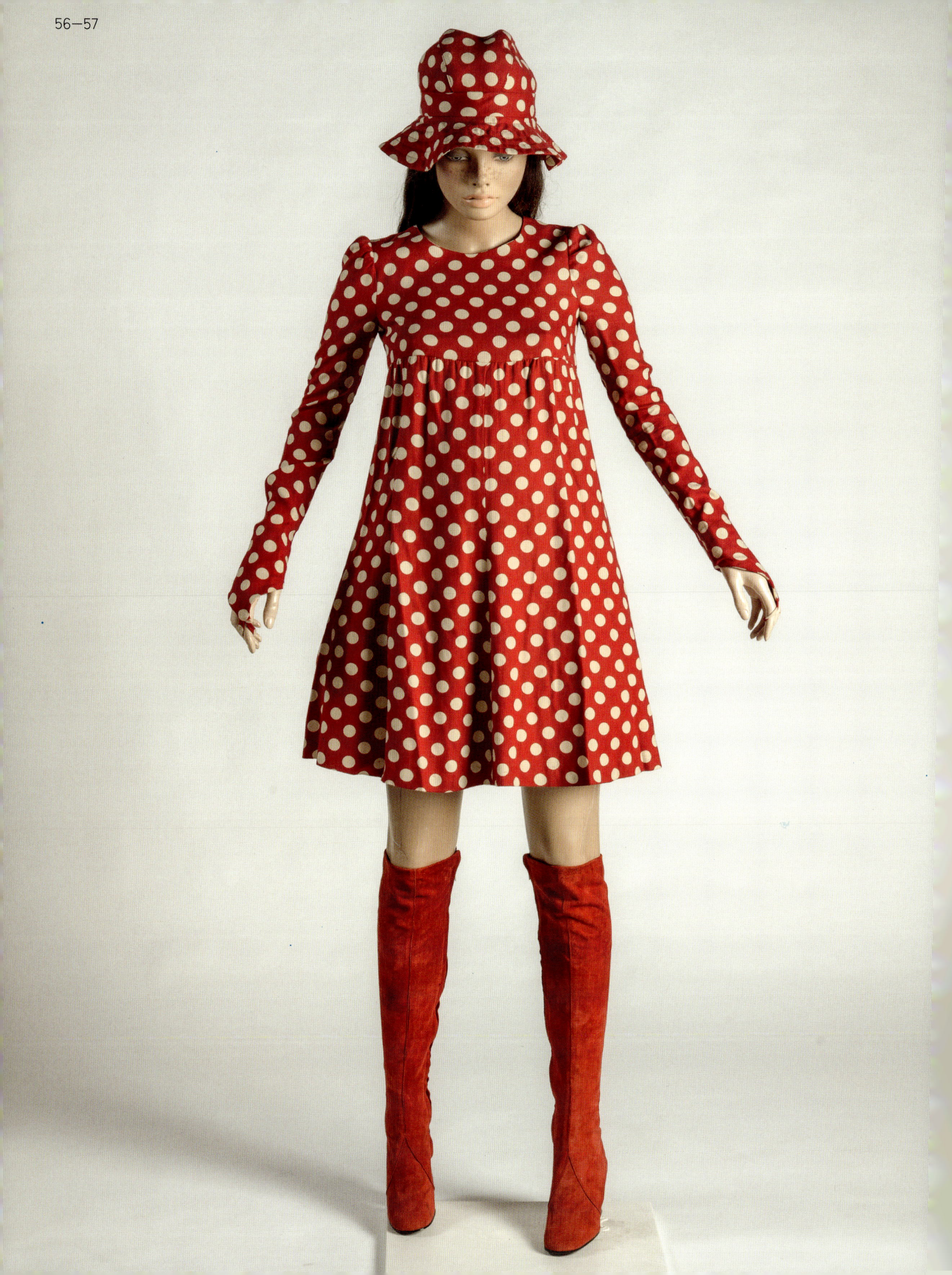

# Biba, Bobby Hillson and Orange Hand

Girl's red and white spotted dress, hat and boots by Biba. Checked cotton dress and pinafore by Bobby Hillson. Boy's ensemble by Orange Hand for Burton

## Chosen by Moira Keenan at *The Sunday Times*

Moira Keenan was one of an inspired team at *The Sunday Times* that had, under the eagle eye of editor Ernestine Carter, transformed the way fashion was portrayed in newsprint, introducing stylish photographers and designers to a far greater readership. *The Sunday Times* fashion pages had a roving remit to, as Ernestine Carter put it, 'discover the best standard of quality, not necessarily based on price, but on excellence of design, creative ability and value'. Her editorial team covered everything from fashion and interior design to children's wear.

Biba was a true fashion democracy, where everybody was catered for in a series of ever-larger premises on Kensington High Street culminating in the one which opened in 1974 at the huge former Derry & Toms department store. Everything from feather boas to food was available within these dimly lit temples to the golden years of Art Nouveau and Art Deco. Barbara Hulanicki's clothes for children met the same standards of design that she invested in the rest of her lines, and the same basic ideals of coordination and affordability. From 1968 a mail order catalogue meant that her designs were available nationwide.

As a distinguished fashion illustrator working in a vaguely Art Nouveau style, Bobby Hillson's pen and ink sketches chimed perfectly with the wide-eyed nostalgic look of the late 1960s and early 1970s, and indeed many adult designs translated perfectly into children's wear. Working initially for *Vogue*, then covering the Paris collections for *The Sunday Times* and *The Observer*, in 1969 she founded her own children's wear firm with journalist Jane Barnicoat. Although relatively short-lived, it produced simple, classic clothes with a nostalgic air, including versions of the smock dresses and shifts she had drawn at the

catwalk shows. After her spell as a designer she turned to teaching, and is credited with establishing an MA course in Fashion Studies at what is now Central Saint Martins.

Orange Hand was Burton's nationwide chain of boy's clothes boutiques, opened in 1972, with the first five branches in Reading, Brighton, Nottingham, Uxbridge and London's Sloane Square. Designed by Foster Associates, and with a neon orange fist as their logo, a distinct identity brought high fashion to a new and untapped market. Each store was fitted with a standard colour scheme of yellow, white and orange, aiming to appeal to an ever-younger fashion-conscious audience. The experiment, whilst stylish and innovative, never turned a profit, and the chain had closed by 1976.

## Shop kit for a roving chain

The Burton Group leaves nothing for the landlord when it moves an Orange Hand boys clothing shop. Ilse Gray explains the mobile concept developed by Foster Associates

*The orange fist symbol is featured as a neon sign on the fascia and screen-printed onto signs above each*

With the omniscient burgeoning of new city shopping centres and the increasing supply of short lease sites, it is foolish for owners of modest-sized chainstores to custom-fit each individual shop.

When Foster Associates was asked by the Burton Group to design and develop five units in an eventual nationwide chain of Orange Hand boys' clothes shops, the practice realised that most chainstores were fitted out on a one-off basis and that the fittings were often

of the opening with a separate suspended flashing neon Orange Hand sign behind it; this too can migrate with the owner and costs half as much as Burton's original fixed sign. Walls and ceiling inside are painted white and the vinyl floor is white too. Foster Associates believes in using all available budget on the development of essentials and not on what they term "cosmetics". Their air handling unit and ductwork for instance is suspended exposed from the

ers so the architect designed an ingenious 6ft long single unit with a basic tube steel frame which can be used either vertically against the wall o horizontally on the floor.

Changing cubicles are made up of units infilled with metal lised acrylic, mirror side out because young customers spend too much time inside admiring themselves. The cash desk is designed as an individual item but its black rubber top and Grattnell drawers make it visually consistent. Sign have been rationalised to a simple system of cards between acrylic sheets bolted together and fixed to the units on black anodised aluminium clamps using allen screws. The sign writing i facilitated by the use of a small printing machine. Sign include a screen-printed Orange Hand symbol.

The initial crash programme for the five shops at Reading Brighton, Nottingham, Uxbridge and London's Sloane Square took five months from research and development stage to shop opening in December last year. Time on site averaged nine weeks. The price for a shop, adding in all development, design, components, site work and even the smallest accessories, was £15,000 which is of course much more than future shops

Orange Hand boutiques were a short-lived but vibrant boys' fashion brand, owned by Burton. *Design* magazine, May 1973

'The very young have probably never been so fashion-conscious, so aware of how every little detail of their dress must be, so absolutely certain of how they must look.'

Moira Keenan

# Christian Dior and Yves Saint Laurent

**White wool coat and matching hat by Jorn Lanberg for Christian Dior's 'Diorling' label. Man's ensemble by Yves Saint Laurent for Rive Gauche**

**Chosen by Alison Adburgham at *The Guardian***

Without doubt two of the brightest stars of 20th-century fashion, both Marc Bohan and Yves Saint Laurent were masters of running couture and ready-to-wear businesses simultaneously. They also shared a link through Christian Dior.

Yves Saint Laurent had already been chosen by Dior as his eventual successor, but the couturier's unexpected death aged 52 meant that Saint Laurent took centre stage sooner than anyone had expected. His debut solo collection for Dior in Spring/Summer 1958 was rapturously received by the press; his skill in refreshing the New Look was self-evident. However, successive collections were increasingly criticised as unwearable or too avant-garde. As a result, Marcel Boussac, the owner of the label, swiftly appointed Marc Bohan to replace Saint Laurent as soon as the latter was conscripted for compulsory military service in 1960.

Transferred to Bohan's shoulders was the weight of one of the world's great and most influential couture houses. So large was the operation that individual design studios produced ranges simultaneously in Paris, London and New York, whilst also running 'Diorling' for younger clients. The simply tailored white wool coat and matching hat of Spring/Summer 1973 were by Jorn Lanberg, head of design at the Christian Dior studios in London, based on Bohan's couture range from the previous season. Typical of the understated luxury associated with Dior at a time, the economic downturn in Europe dictated that the days of many exclusive ateliers and couture salons were numbered.

Yves Saint Laurent opened his own couture label in 1962 and Rive Gauche in 1966. The label was aimed at the quality ready-to-wear market, one which the

designer rapidly realised could be just as lucrative as his couture lines. This was one of the most intensely creative periods of Saint Laurent's history. 1966 saw the introduction of masculine tailoring with 'Le Smoking', a woman's version of the tuxedo, 1969 brought the Safari look and, perhaps most influentially, there was the celebrated 'Russian' collection of 1976. Rive Gauche quickly diversified into perfume, make-up and accessories, even cigarettes, largely spurred on by Saint Laurent's astute partner Pierre Bergé.

Seen together, the 1973 outfits offer the very best of a pared-down, luxurious and yet modern vision of dressing; casual, cool and sophisticated.

# 1974

# Missoni

**Male and female knitted ensembles, shoes by Pasquali**

**Chosen by Jennifer Hocking at *Harpers & Queen***

Husband and wife team Ottavio and Rosita founded Missoni in Italy in 1953, and by the time of the 1974 Dress of the Year Award they were often mentioned in the same breath as Gucci and Louis Vuitton as the last word in Italian luxury.

Like Bill Gibb, they specialised in luxurious craft, and in the combination of vibrant colours, patterns and textures. Their designs were championed by Emmanuelle Khanh (with whom they collaborated in 1966) and, most importantly for their international profile, Diana Vreeland at American *Vogue*. In London, Joan and Sidney Burstein selected Missoni for Brown's, their influential boutique on South Molton Street, and Jennifer Hocking's readers at *Harpers & Queen* would have approved of her choice of a heavily 1920s-influenced ensemble.

At the time of the award, Jennifer Hocking's reasons for selecting the duo were simple: 'Inspired by the ever-changing colours of his local countryside, Ottavio Missoni designs almost living, breathing colours, textures and patterns – in fabrics that range from the finest featherweight silk jersey to the thickest, softest mohair. Rosita Missoni then shapes these superb fabrics into shirts, skirts, dresses, trousers and capes, all of them interchangeable in an endless, heady permutation of colour ... beautiful, luxurious clothes that fit town or country landscape ... in fact, collector's items.'

Both outfits owe much of their inspiration to the inter-war period, from the clever use of fabric on the cross and the draped layers of the female ensemble, to the shawl-collared cardigan and wide, straight-cut trousers of the man's. However, in their clever use of colour, patchwork segments, textures and layers of weaves they successfully avoid direct pastiche. Accessorised with the glamorous shoes of Guido Pasquali, 1974 was an all-Italian affair. The bold 'correspondent' shoes and demure crossover strapped sandals continued the Jazz Age theme personified by Robert Redford and Mia Farrow in the film of F Scott Fitzgerald's novel *The Great Gatsby,* released the same year.

Chosen with the ensemble was Adel Rootstein's mannequin of model Marie Helvin, at the time muse to David Bailey, and one of the most enduring models of the late 20th century.

'The Missonis live and work in a small village some forty miles from Milan, and from that small Italian village the influence of this astonishing design team has spread to inspire awe and envy in the fashion business throughout the world.'

Jennifer Hocking

# Gina Fratini and Tommy Nutter

Cream silk organza wedding ensemble by Gina Fratini, eau de Nil frock coat with moiré silk lapels by Tommy Nutter, green glacé leather brogues by The Chelsea Cobbler

Chosen by Anna Harvey at *Brides* magazine

'Gina Fratini designs the prettiest clothes one can buy ... Tommy Nutter is not gimmicky but imaginative, and prepared to be adventurous.'

Anna Harvey

If romance was in the air, Gina Fratini had the perfect dress to fulfil every bride's dream. By the late 1960s, and perhaps as a direct reaction to the stark and angular modernism of the mini-skirt, designers like Bill Gibb and Gina Fratini looked to the past to inspire their vision of idealised, historically influenced clothes.

Since showing her first collection in 1966, she had created a hallmark look of layered gauze, pretty prints, petticoats edged in lace or broderie anglaise, high-necked empire line dresses with fitted sleeves, and frilled cuffs. By the early 1970s the Gina Fratini look merged fantasy with reality: gowns became full-scale romantic extravaganzas, with huge skirts and layers of luxury silks and satins, often accessorised with a flower basket or gathered fabric drawstring purse, as in the case of the 1975 Dress of the Year. 'Her dresses will become heirlooms and be handed down through the family, as they will never date', was Anna Harvey's view.

If Gina Fratini's bride looked as though she had stepped from the pages of a romantic novel, then Tommy Nutter's bridegroom was her dandy in a frock coat, as not even men's tailoring was left untouched by this romantic revival. Worn with a ruffled white stock at the neck, the outfit is loosely based on late 19th-century morning dress; in pale eau de Nil, it offers a refreshing alternative to tradition whilst balancing Gina Fratini's extravaganza to perfection.

By opening up his Savile Row workrooms with windows on to the street, Tommy Nutter had brought boutique retailing to a bastion of tradition, and like Fratini he shared a passion for the past. His first boutique opened in 1968 and by the early 1970s he was revisiting the classic tailoring of the 1930s with Gatsby hats, Norfolk jackets and plus-fours. He combined patterns in innovative ways, mixing different scales of check and herringbone, and accessorising with bright waistcoats and 'correspondent' shoes from the likes of The Chelsea Cobbler.

# 1976

## Kenzo and Fiorucci

Two coordinated printed cotton dresses by Kenzo Takada for Jap, man's jeans and hand-knitted sweater by Elio Fiorucci

Chosen by Helena Matheopoulos at the *Daily Express*

'Fashion in the mid-seventies can be summed up as "The age of Jap".'

Helena Matheopoulos

The vibrant prints and simple, functional tailoring of Japan were the hallmark of Kenzo Takada, a double Dress of the Year winner who had relocated from Tokyo to Paris in the mid-1960s. There he opened the boutique Jungle Jap, adapting the wrap-round style of the kimono for modern European clothing. His simple lines and user-friendly styles became an instant hit, combining clashes and coordination in equal measure. Introduced to London by boutique owner Joseph Ettedgui, Kenzo clothes were relaxed, functional and fun, startling the fashion world by presenting relaxed 'peasant' styles in printed floral and plain cottons when many other designers were concentrating on re-working the sophistication of the 1930s.

First shown in his collection for Spring/Summer 1976, the 'hip-wrap' became an instant hit, as did the simple tunic, both chosen for Dress of the Year 1976.

Milan's Fiorucci shop was the talk of Italy, a brash and bright retailer in the heart of sedate sophistication. Their jeans for men and women were as popular in Europe as they were in the discos of Manhattan. London's Fiorucci boutique opened in autumn 1975, channelling the energies of a team of designers into clothes for a young and casual clientele with more than a hint of humour. In a similar vein to Tommy Roberts' Mr Freedom boutique in Kensington, which operated earlier in the decade, the core clientele enjoyed the brand's irreverent nostalgia for all things 1950s. By the mid-1970s Elio Fiorucci's empire had spread across the globe, with provocative advertising campaigns employing the imagery of the glamorous 1940s pin-up girls of Alberto Vargas.

The Dress of the Year 1976 ensembles were originally modelled on a trio of Rootstein's new black mannequins. This was an acknowledgement of the increasing success of contemporary superstar models such as Pat Cleveland, Donyale Luna and Beverly Johnson, the last being the first African-American woman to appear on the cover of US *Vogue* just two years earlier.

# Kenzo

Khaki cotton dress, straw hat and plimsolls
by Kenzo Takada for Kenzo

Chosen by Ann Boyd at *The Observer*

'The man who got us into longer skirts has reintroduced the mini. Practically no one else could have done it.'

Ann Boyd

Just as the fashion world was becoming accustomed to both Kenzo Takada's success and his ankle-skimming tied and wrapped print dresses, he changed tack and reintroduced the mini – not as the tapering shift of the previous decade, but as a short and sharp belted shirt dress. Referencing the khaki of military uniforms, which had first invaded the catwalks of Paris with Yves Saint Laurent in the late 1960s, Kenzo's Winter 1976/7 collection included tiny wrap mini-skirts shown with shorts, and chunky jumper dresses worn over ribbed tights.

Ann Boyd commented: 'Kenzo's new mini is a much more relaxed garment than its '60s ancestor. The new mini, Jap style, is a big shirt, and its beauty is that for the daring it can be worn on its own, or for the more feeble-minded it can be just as successful with trousers or a skirt. Here worn at its more daring, with flat canvas shoes and rolled ankle socks, it is the epitome of Kenzo's '70s mini. Kenzo has given us mixed patterns, bright colours, giant sweaters, long skirts, the African look, the Chinese look, layers, and finally the '70s mini.'

The previous Spring/Summer 1976 Kenzo collection had been his greatest coup to date. It earned him his first Dress of the Year award and could arguably be credited with giving fashion a whole new direction. Now, his relaxed, cross-coordinated khakis carried with them a spirit of the new casual clothes which ran throughout the 1970s. As Ann Boyd commented at the time, these were clothes specifically designed for 'mucking around in'. His look was instantly and lastingly successful, and it firmly held its own as an alternative to the nostalgia-orientated clothes of the previous decade.

So influential was the Japanese invasion of the catwalk, that one of the most popular ranges of mannequins by Adel Rootstein at the time was of Japanese models. In this case the mannequin featured is 'Sayoko', named after catwalk sensation Sayoko Yamaguchi.

# 1978

# Gordon Luke Clarke and Cerruti

Printed cotton tunic, skirt and trousers, worn with black leather skirt and coat by Gordon Luke Clarke. Men's ensemble in wool and tweed by Lucien Foncel for Cerruti

Chosen by Barbara Griggs at the *Daily Mail*

Barbara Griggs was less than impressed by fashion in general in 1977, commenting: 'I suspect few women will look back on the typical fashions of 1977 with any real regret. As interpreted by the leading designers in Paris, Milan and London, the line was big, baggy and bulky; the colours were subdued if not dreary. It suited few women; it pleased few men.' In her eyes, however, there were two exceptions: Gordon Luke Clarke and Cerruti. 'In this non-vintage year these two designers stand out like beacons for me. New Zealander Gordon Luke Clarke is designing the prettiest women's clothes imaginable whilst Cerruti, oldest-established French menswear house, now revived by a superb designer, Lucien Foncel, is turning out superb off-the-peg clothes for men and women.'

The owner of Luke's boutique in Chelsea, Gordon Luke Clarke had only just launched his collection of separates before landing his Dress of the Year award. He sold simple, sexy, versatile shapes in soft, permanently pleated fabric, printed in dazzling mixes of pure colour and meant to be switched, mixed and matched. His typical client was the modern working woman who, whilst not afraid to spend generously on her wardrobe, expected versatility and staying-power as standard. 'They're clothes that give huge fun to their wearer, huge pleasures to the beholder; and if that isn't what fashion is about, tell it to the buyers that jam pack Gordon's stand at the London Fashion Fair every season,' was Barbara Griggs' comment.

With his elegant ensemble in subtle tweed and wool, Lucien Foncel at Cerruti went some way in covering the ground lost by French menswear to Italian and American designers over the previous decade. Barbara Griggs was unreservedly enthusiastic: 'He has restored our faith in elegance for menswear. His eye for colour never falters – particularly important in the limited palette of male dress, and his cut is masterly – soft, immensely comfortable but innately stylish. If I were a rich man, his are the clothes I'd want to wear all the time.'

'Gordon Luke Clarke and Cerruti epitomise the cleverly put together, multi-layered, mixed and matched ingenuity of present day fashion trends.'

Barbara Griggs

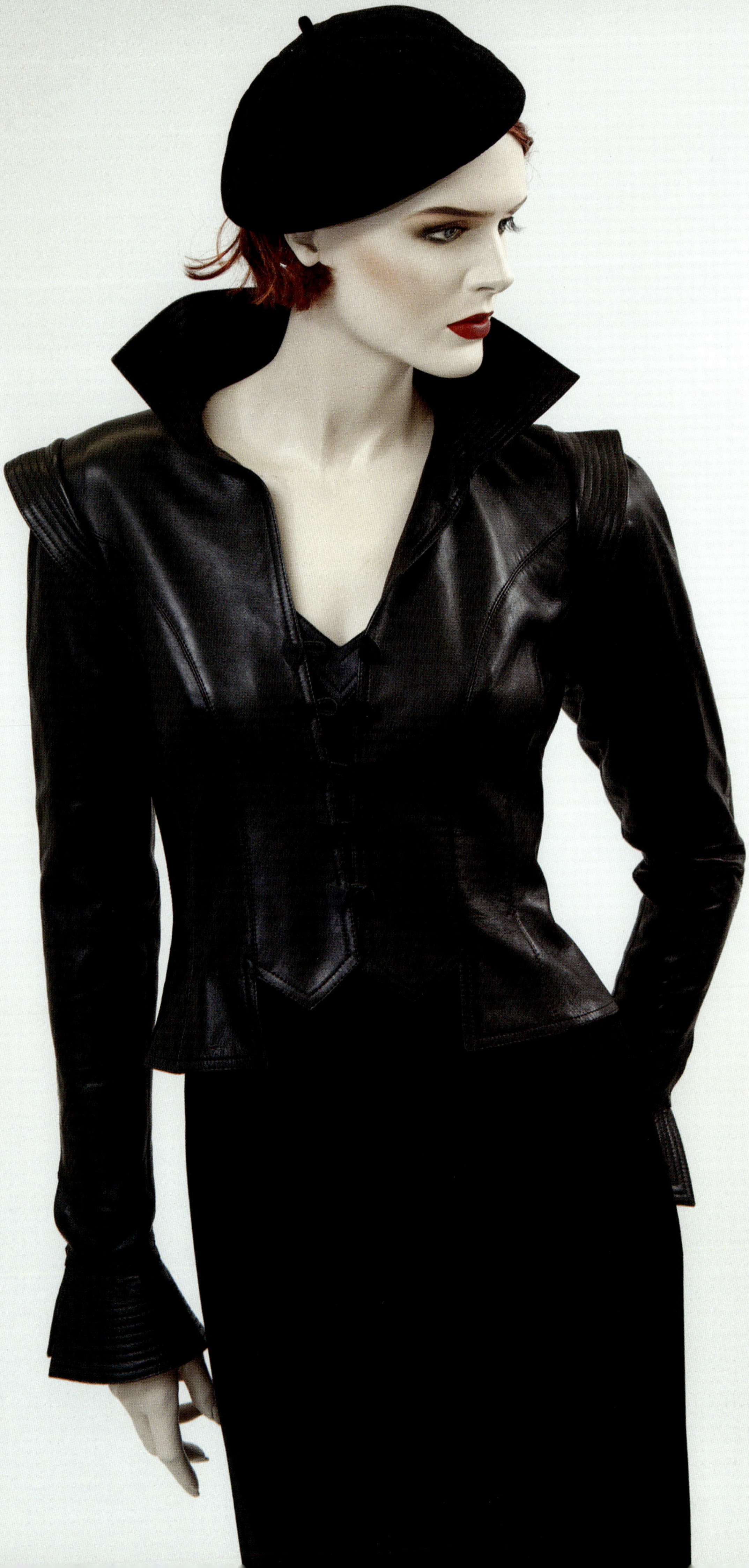

# Jean Muir

Black rayon jersey dress, beret and tailored black leather jacket, shoes by Manolo Blahnik for Zapata

Chosen by Geraldine Ranson at *The Sunday Telegraph*

THE SUNDAY TELEGRAPH    SEPTEMBER 2, 1979

## My dress of the year

### BY GERALDINE RANSON

IF you were asked to pick The Dress of the Year, what would you choose? This was the problem that Bath City Council set when they invited me to select a dress to represent 1979 for their Museum of Costume. By way of direction, they added that I could choose absolutely anything from any designer anywhere.

I knew it would have to be a dress that I really loved. Then I tried to imagine my great-granddaughter with her own child in the museum working out how great-granny looked. What image did I want to leave? I decided I wanted her to see the best and most elegant fashion that Britain could make and the one British designer today above all others whose dresses are prized and admired across the world. So I chose Jean Muir.

Every great designer has a golden age and I believe that these are Jean's vintage years.

The dress and jacket I have chosen are in two materials not often used together but which Jean uses with total mastery: matt rayon jersey and leather. Neither material is easy to handle but here they are cut and sewn with great skill.

If my great-granddaughter is perceptive, she will be able to draw certain conclusions from this and previous exhibits. Perhaps the most important changes in recent years have been the deceleration in the change of fashion coupled with a frightening rate of inflation. As a result women are spending more and buying less; they are shopping very carefully and buying clothes to wear for several seasons. Inevitably, fashion has become more classic, responding as it does to the mood of the times.

The second important conclusion my descendant might draw is that sporty shapes have moved into evening clothes. The black leather fencing jacket here is a prime example. To look *endimanché* is to be unfashionable.

From tomorrow the dress and jacket will be on permanent exhibition at The Museum of Costume, Assembly Rooms, Bennet Street, Bath. The museum is open daily from 9.30 am to 6.00 pm (10.00 am to 5.00 pm November 1 to March 1) except Christmas and Boxing Day, and admission is 80p. For the next week the dress can be seen in the window of Harvey Nichols, Knightsbridge, London, SW1.

*Jean Muir*

LEFT: Matt rayon dress with leather-trimmed V-neck and long sleeves, £174. Nappa leather fencing jacket, £319. Both in black only, in sizes 8 to 14 by Jean Muir. From Harvey Nichols, Knightsbridge, London, SW1; Olive Walton, Birmingham. Black suede shoes by Manolo Blahnik for Zapata, 49/51 Old Church Street, London, SW3.

Sketch by Helen Florence

Geraldine Ranson profiled her choice of Jean Muir for *The Sunday Telegraph* in September 1979.

Eleven years after her first award, Jean Muir proved her enduring skill by returning as winner of Dress of the Year with her lean and supremely elegant jersey dress, worn with a fitted short jacket and matching beret. Her look for the close of the decade predicted a return to the sleek and sophisticated dressing of the film noir heroine, the femme fatale of black and white films. Her reputation for the skilful use of jersey was to carry her business internationally, and it was something she adapted here to work in leather, creating the nipped-in waist of the jacket.

Geraldine Ranson relished the challenge of choosing the Dress of the Year. 'I knew it would have to be a dress that I really loved. Then I tried to imagine my own great-granddaughter with her own child in the museum, working out how great grannie looked. I decided I wanted her to see the best and most elegant fashion Britain could produce, and the one British designer whose dresses are prized and admired across the world. So I chose Jean Muir.'

Neither material is easy to handle, but they are cut and sewn with great skill. At a time of pronounced economic recession, she argued that women were forced to spend more to buy less, so that a market naturally emerged for classic, timeless clothes. Here the jacket, retailing at £310, is loosely inspired by a fitted fencing jacket. The matt rayon jersey dress sold for £174.

Manolo Blahnik operated Zapata from a small but beautifully formed boutique in Chelsea's Old Church Street, a location which still survives to this day as the only stand-alone Manolo Blahnik boutique in London. From there he joined a celebrated, and notably small, group of designers, comprising Terry de Havilland, The Chelsea Cobbler and Anello and Davide, to provide London's fashionable feet with exquisite shoes. All four designers shared longevity in the fashion footwear business, based largely on a combination of both design and business talent.

'Every great designer has a golden age and I believe these are Jean's vintage years.'

Geraldine Ranson 1979

'The designer sees the wearer herself moulding the dress to her own requirements, rather than the dress imposing the shape of fashion on her.'

Dress of the Year Press Release

# Calvin Klein

Red and brown striped silk dress with leather belt, worn with wooden jewellery, shoes by Diego Della Valle

Chosen by Michael Roberts at *The Sunday Times*

An all-American invasion of the world's catwalks began in the late 1970s with designers like Calvin Klein, who perfected the art of providing simple, elegant clothes, selling and refining the American dream.

Chosen by style writer and accomplished fashion illustrator Michael Roberts, the Dress of the Year 1980 marks the point at which fashion polarised, and told a variety of different stories over the next decade. Calvin Klein was the original 'Native New Yorker', frequenting New York nightclub Studio 54 and selling his world-famous blue jeans to the world in smash-hit advertising campaigns starring a young Brooke Shields. He embraced the changes in working patterns that saw a growing need for extended working wardrobes for women; by 1980 his look was evolving into the classic preppy America of Long Island, the Hamptons and Yale, reworking formal European tradition for modern Americans.

In striped silk, this simple dress could be worn night or day, formalised with jewellery or worn loose and free. Function dictated form for the modern woman, with the press release at the time noting that 'the model's hair is cut in a short, natural style that looks both natural and sleek. The dress is intended to be suitable for a number of different social occasions and for women of different ages.'

Teamed with burgundy leather strap sandals by Diego Della Valle, founder of the brand Tod's, the very best of US fashion met classic Italian shoe design with a similar brand image. Founded in the early 1970s, Tod's was specifically associated with the US and sold to department stores across the country, retaining handmade quality whilst selling its famed driving shoes in large quantities.

Like Calvin Klein, Tod's target audience was the stylish, modern American who appreciated quality as much as versatility.

# 1981

## Karl Lagerfeld for Chloé

White silk crêpe-de-chine evening dress with bold print, worn with flat red patent shoes with mesh inserts, also by Chloé, and jewellery by Ugo Correani

Chosen by Vanessa de Lisle at *Harpers & Queen*

An invitation to the unveiling of the Dress of the Year award for 1981, sponsored by *Harpers & Queen*.

Before his move to Chanel in 1983, Karl Lagerfeld had managed to achieve a remarkable selection of roles. Amongst other houses, he worked for Pierre Balmain, Jean Patou, Chloé and Krizia. With Chloé since 1966 as head designer, his chameleon qualities had enabled him to produce successive collections that adhered to founder Gaby Aghion's ideal of producing couture-quality clothes for the ready-to-wear market.

The Chloé hallmark of soft, fluid clothes had been immensely popular throughout the previous decade and by 1981, print was at the forefront of Lagerfeld's collection. In the case of the Dress of the Year it was a boldly coloured abstract leaf design on white silk crêpe-de-chine, by the designer himself.

Selector Vanessa de Lisle wrote: 'His collections over many years have never faltered; he is the one designer who knows how to make a dress that will look good on the wearer. He uses the most simple lines always – a softly rolled draped boat neckline is a tremendously simple look that flatters any face, and it is carried through to the rolled and padded hemline and the rolled finish to the sleeves.'

At a time of a dramatically changed political landscape in Britain, she also sensed a new enjoyment in smart dressing for the evening: '1981 is the "after-six" year in Britain without a doubt; retrenchment politically always leads to formality in dressing, and the women who might have worn jeans and a silk shirt to go out to dinner a year or so ago are now dressing much more carefully after dark.'

Originally shown on a Rootstein mannequin of fashion model Victoria Robinson, and worn with coral jewellery by Ugo Correani.

'Karl Lagerfeld has always had a rhythm
of his own. He is a designer, in his collections
for Chloé, who epitomises more than any
other, the sense of being beautifully dressed.'

Vanessa de Lisle

# 1982

# Margaret Howell and Nigel Preston

Linen skirt, waistcoat and shirt by Margaret Howell. Blue suede and fawn chamois leather skirt, jacket and cotton shirt by Nigel Preston at Maxfield Parrish. Shoes by Manolo Blahnik for Zapata, belts by Mulberry

Chosen by Grace Coddington at British *Vogue*

Grace Coddington had been a successful model in the 'Young Ideas' section of British *Vogue* before, under the watchful eye of Beatrix Miller, joining the magazine as a young fashion editor in 1968. By 1982 she was senior fashion editor, and her choice of Margaret Howell typified the new generation of simple, elegant clothes produced in the eighties as just one of the many fashion stories unfolding, eminently suitable for work or play, exhibiting a pared-down masculine simplicity.

With experience of supplying her shirts to both Ralph Lauren and Paul Smith since the mid-1970s, Margaret Howell designed her first womenswear collection in 1980. Her look was layered, fluid and easy to wear, match and coordinate, emphasising simplicity of style in linen, cottons and silks. At the time of the award Grace Coddington commented: 'Margaret Howell's style has evolved over the years; a perfectionist, unaffected by her contemporaries, she designs with an excellent eye for detail and function. She began by making men's clothes, successfully adapting them for women while maintaining their traditional quality and cut.'

The designer has said of her work, 'I think of myself as a hands-on designer. For me, make is integral to my design philosophy. It is crucial how a piece of clothing feels when worn. I've always wanted clothes to be the way I drew them – relaxed and lived-in, a natural look. I find men's clothes interesting in their structure, feel and functionality. I started by designing men's clothes, and then found that women wanted them' (www.margarethowell.co.uk/story).

Of Nigel Preston, Grace Coddington was equally effusive. 'Women appreciate the almost 'un-designed' elegance of his suedes, which allows them to assert their individuality. He uses suede like fabric, and the result is a casual simplicity which makes his clothes ideal alone, but versatile to mix in with any like-minded fashion – a Margaret Howell shirt for example. His skill is outstanding in a year noted for the importance of suede.'

He named his boutique on the King's Road after his favourite artist, and from Maxfield Parrish he was widely credited with rehabilitating contemporary fashion's perception of leather and suede – making them, once again, desirable.

'At one of the most highly competitive times in fashion history these are two designers who successfully represent British talent worldwide. They have their own distinctive styles and have consistently concentrated on what they do best.'

Grace Coddington

# 1983

## Sheridan Barnett

Linen dress and coat, shoes by Manolo Blahnik

**Chosen by Sally Brampton at *The Observer***

With a career that ranges from pattern-grading with Ossie Clark to designing for Quorum, Jaeger, Norman Hartnell and his own label, Sheridan Barnett produced practical, layered and easy-to-wear clothes; the wardrobe of the liberated working 1980s woman.

In a decade noted for extremes, his fashion was all about a subtle, unassuming sophistication. Sally Brampton chose the Dress of the Year for precisely these reasons, and noted, 'The looks for 1983 are, according to the international designers, as disparate as possible, ranging from the loose layered lines adored by the Japanese designers, presently hailed as the new fashion messiahs, to the slick tailored chic of the Parisians.'

'Sheridan Barnett's clothes are particularly expressive of the confident woman of the '80s. Less concerned with the traditional feminist role of aggressively burning her bra or striking a coyly liberated pose, she is happy to wear clothes which are not obviously stereotyped. The dress of '83 reflects this attitude of relaxed confidence. The effect is one of fluidity and movement that relies more on the confidence of the body beneath it to give it life, than on structured tailoring or fancy ornament.'

The influence of this updated shirt dress is reflected in the fact that it was endlessly copied by the ready-to-wear market across the UK at the time. Fashion brands such as Principles, Next, Wallis and Richards Shops all developed extended working wardrobes for women using the same combination of simplicity of line and textures found in the 1983 Dress of the Year.

One of his greatest fans was fashion writer Brenda Polan, who commented the following year: 'His fondness for menswear fabrics and shapes combined with his preference for sweeping, dramatic proportions was, and still is, a major influence on world fashion.'

'There are no such things as "in" or "out" now; instead there are many and acceptable varying trends. Sheridan Barnett has never deviated from his belief in the simplicity of practical clothing and the purity of modern, almost architectural, design.'

Ann Boyd

Opposite page
Evangelina Blahnik wears the 1983
Dress of the Year, including shoes
by her brother Manolo.

# 1984

## David Holah and Stevie Stewart at Body Map, Betty Jackson and Katharine Hamnett

Coordinating skirt, jumper, stockings, hat and waxed jacket by Body Map. Dress, cardigan, hat and scarf by Betty Jackson. Slogan T-shirt and cotton trousers by Katharine Hamnett

Chosen by Brenda Polan at *The Guardian*

Three of Britain's cult labels of the 1980s were Brenda Polan's fashion heroes for 1984.

David Holah and Stevie Stewart at Body Map defined the mid-eighties with their fresh approach to cutting and inspired use of layered fabrics and knits. In business since 1982, and via a stall in Camden Market, they injected a totally new feel into clothing for the young, combining graphic designs by Hilde Smith with long, lean, stretched and baggy silhouettes, and hallmark dropped waists. Their clothes were smart and casual in equal measure, and an instant hit on the clubbing scene.

A rebel with a cause, Katharine Hamnett's 1983 'Choose Life' collection of slogan T-shirts politicised fashion, and were some of the most memorable design statements of the decade. Slogans included 'Education Not Missiles' and '58% Don't Want Pershing', one of which she famously wore to a 1984 Downing Street reception for fashion designers in the presence of Margaret Thatcher. Brenda Polan was a particular fan of her menswear, stating at the time of her award: 'Katharine's clothes for men, which are very similar to her clothes for women, played a major part, along with those of her colleagues Margaret Howell, Paul Smith and Scott Crolla and Georgina Godley, in opening a space for the rest of the revitalised menswear industry to walk through. This year British fashion has established itself even more securely as the fount of all new ideas, off which the worldwide industry is feeding. Indeed, it is fair to say that not even in the sixties did Britain see such a rich flowering of creative talent, such a sense of excitement, purpose and success.'

Betty Jackson shared a brief stint designing for Quorum alongside other Dress of the Year winners Ossie Clark and Sheridan Barnett. Her hallmark style blends a fluid, casual look with the use of vibrant prints, something to which the designer still adheres today: 'I remember the award was most prestigious and I was surprised and delighted to be a recipient. It came right at the beginning, when we had taken the decision to have a first solo fashion show, and when we began to get international recognition on a much bigger scale. The timing was important as it was a hugely positive comment on the collection by Brenda Polan, who was Women's Editor of *The Guardian* at the time, and very influential. She has remained a staunch supporter throughout.' (Correspondence with the author, January 2013.)

Brenda Polan commented, of Betty Jackson's hallmark style: 'Her big-shouldered, long, lean silhouette and her preference for massive, butch footwear worn with socks is now in evidence at every level of the market'. She cited her reasons for the award, saying: 'Three strands of current fashion are drawn together; Hamnett's brilliant development of comfortable workwear, Jackson's sure senses of colour and sinuous line, an approach to dress both classy and sexy which few designers are able to synthesise, and Body Map's raunchy ebullience, their beautifully controlled expression of a vital, mostly light-hearted youth culture, a phenomenon which is entirely British.'

BROWN and lime asymmetrical striped long dress worn with Hush Puppies and socks by Betty Jackson

Betty Jackson's original design for an 'asymmetrical long dress worn with Hush Puppies and socks'.
Betty Jackson archive

'They have in common a sense of fluidity and ease, a superb and daring colour sense, a fresh conception of proportion and, above all, an ability to invest their clothes with an almost tangible sense of aliveness, excitement and humour.'

Brenda Polan

The *Guardian* fashion editor Brenda Polan was this year's judge of The Dress of the Year Award, sponsored by the Museum of Costume, Bath. The prize is awarded to a dress or outfit which best reflects influential ideas in contemporary fashion.
Seen here is Brenda Polan and Betty Jackson (left) with her prize winning design. Other recipients of the award were BodyMap and Katharine Hamnett.

Brenda Polan, fashion editor of *The Guardian*, congratulates Betty Jackson (left) on winning Dress of the Year in 1984 along with Katharine Hamnett and Bodymap.

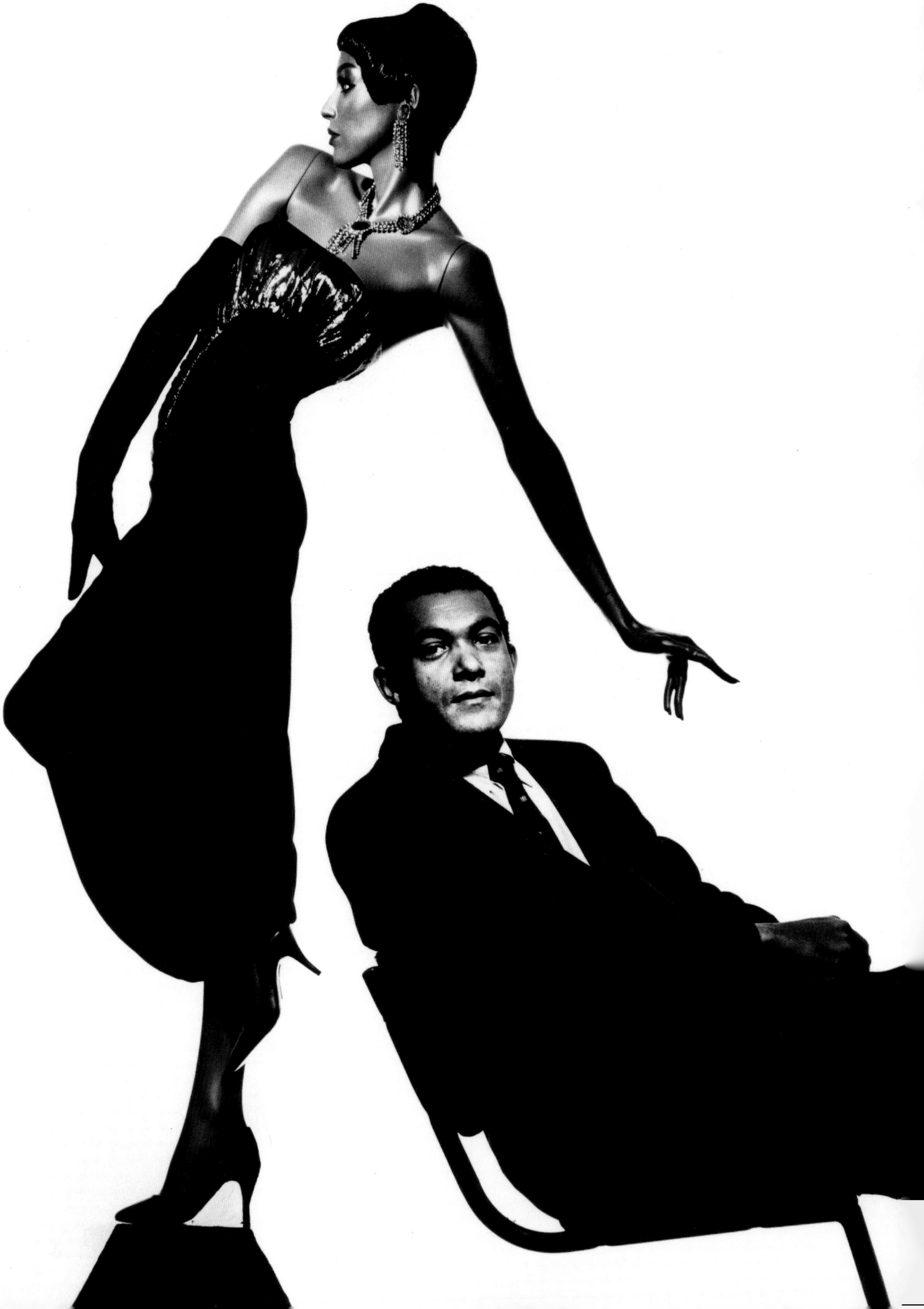

# 1985

# Bruce Oldfield
## and Scott Crolla

Evening dress in black silk and gold lamé by
Bruce Oldfield, shoes by Charles Jourdan, jewellery
by Marla Buck. Shirt, crushed velvet trousers and
ikat mules by Scott Crolla

Chosen by Suzy Menkes at *The Times*

Bruce Oldfield's hallmark of glamorous, sculpted
silhouettes teamed with luxurious use of fabrics
made him one of the great British success stories
of the 1980s.

The glamorous, sophisticated, aspirational 1980s
were personified by Bruce Oldfield's evening wear,
worn by stars of stage and screen and by the late
Diana, Princess of Wales. Often described as 'the
world's most famous Barnardo's boy', his career
could not have had more humble beginnings, but he
has remained at the top of his game for almost 30
years, selling a very particular brand of luxury from
his Beauchamp Place boutique.

In 1985 the Bruce Oldfield signature was the sculpted,
body-hugging sheath dress, often with elements of
metallic lamé. Tailored into the figure, a gentle
S-shaped seam across the front, with gathered fabric
to the upper side, recalls the Hollywood glamour of a
bygone age. The look is as polished and perfect as
the promotional photograph of the designer with his
creation, shot for Suzy Menkes at *The Times*. In 1986
he, along with other fashion houses such as Mondi
and Louis Féraud, provided clothing for the hit drama
*Howards' Way*, the BBC's attempt to emulate the
style and success of America's *Dallas* and *Dynasty*.
Oldfield's particular kind of smart tailored suits, draped
cocktail dresses and statement evening gowns were
perfectly suited for this, whether it be a society
wedding or a high-powered business meeting.

Scott Crolla applied a similar glamour to menswear
with his glittering brocade patchwork shirt and
sumptuous ruby velvet trousers, the likes of which
had not been seen in London since the late 1960s.
The inspiration in this case came from the luxurious
brocades and velvets of the Middle East, and in
partnership with Georgina Godley he established a
boutique just off Savile Row, the original home of
the 'Piccadilly Peacocks' almost 20 years earlier.
'It's an image of an Englishman with all his traditional
arrogance and confidence who doesn't give a damn
about dressing as long as he assembles all the right
elements. It was meant to be a total assault in taste',
he commented in an interview with Suzy Menkes for
*The Times*, March 1985.

Scott Crolla brought exotic and luxurious fabric back to menswear, the likes of which had not been seen in London since the Savile Row boutiques of Mr Fish and Blades in the late 1960s.

'It is for his skills as a dressmaker, for
his belief in cut, line and silhouette,
for his standards of workmanship and
for his conception of women that I choose
Bruce Oldfield. For fathering the idea
of the peacock male... Scott Crolla.'

Suzy Menkes

# 1986

## Giorgio Armani

Checked wool jacket and skirt worn with black suede shoes. Jacket, trousers and shirt worn with brogues

Chosen by Colin McDowell at *Country Life*

### By Colin McDowell

The Earl of Lichfield ... Michael Roberts ... and me. No wonder I felt so honoured to be asked to choose the Dress of the Year for 1986. Only two other men had ever been asked to do it. But there was more to the honour than that: at the time I was not exactly working for a mainstream fashion publication as most of the previously chosen journalists were. I was fashion editor of *Country Life* – the very expression seemed to many to be a contradiction in terms. But I knew they were wrong. Under the benign and always intelligent direction and interest of the editor, Marcus Binney (sadly removed by the powers that be), I had my moments of glory. To disprove the common belief that the extent of interest that *County Life* readers had in fashion was finding the bigger and better windproof jacket, I had actually managed to get two fashion covers – one of a Ralph Lauren dress photographed in Culzean Castle and the other a runway close-up shot of a belt. I was saddened that they resulted in quite a lot of cancelled subscriptions but proud that I had already managed to get Rei Kawakubo and Yohji Yamamoto on those august pages before the new editor's tastes forced me to flee.

But, in fact, my choice for Bath was none of those designers. I had worked as a designer in Italy for almost ten years during the seventies, enjoying the heady freedoms and pleasures of Rome, at that time a hedonist's paradise and one which, looking back, seemed able to be enjoyed to the full with next to no money at all. But I didn't just learn how to enjoy myself. I also learned a very great deal about design from close exposure to the work of some of the great masters of the second half of the 20th century: Gianni Versace, Gianfranco Ferré and, above all Giorgio Armani, the only one still alive and working today. For me, although I loved everything that Yves Saint Laurent did, the only truly modern and forward-looking designer at that time was Armani. Also, I admired the skill with which he designed clothes for both sexes with equal fluidity, elegance and authority.

Writer, designer and journalist Colin McDowell with models wearing ensembles by Giorgio Armani, the Dress of the Year winner for 1986, who brought his signature Italian chic to business wear.

I look at my choice today with the benefit of hindsight and I know that I made the right decision. Giorgio Armani was the man who made the Italian Miracle happen and his stature has remained throughout his long and powerful career. His position in fashion history is assured, as indeed is the past and future of the Dress of the Year initiative.

# 1987

## John Galliano

Checked cotton skirt, shirt and coat, worn with a tilt hat, shoes by Patrick Cox

Chosen by Debbi Mason at *Elle*

The designer and model photographed in Bath in 1988. Galliano went on to design for both his own label and ultimately, after a brief period at Givenchy, for the house of Dior in Paris.

Following pages
John Galliano's vision of fashion was complete; his winning 1987 ensemble came to the Fashion Museum accompanied by a lavishly produced folder of promotional drawings and literature, explaining the inspiration for that year's Autumn/Winter collection.
Fashion Museum/John Galliano

Like fellow Dress of the Year winners Jean-Paul Gaultier and Alexander McQueen, the genius of John Galliano lies in his ability to subvert art-historical styles, turning the familiar and nostalgic into something challenging and brand new. In 1987 he flirted with the gathered, swagged and structured tailoring of the late Victorian era, somehow managing to combine it with exotic influences of Frida Kahlo, Latin America and a touch of Gothic. He produced something immediately original and highly influential.

At 25, and only three years after leaving St Martin's School of Art (now Central Saint Martins), Galliano's career was about to go global. His 1987 Spring/Summer collection, shown in London, earned him the coveted Designer of the Year award. The first of his collections in 1984, based on the 18th-century costumes for *Les Incroyables*, was immediately snapped up by influential London boutique owner Joan Burstein for the windows of Browns on South Molton Street. Backing was a perennial problem and at the time of the Dress of the Year award, the John Galliano label had just been rescued by businessman Peder Bertelsen, after a previous mentor withdrew support almost overnight.

In his promotional literature for the collection, Galliano's style is summarised as 'Stamen torsos cupped like fragile bodices as strong and poised as a cut stem. The hems blown up like so many petals caught in the wind and the lengths of the tulip skirts gathered like flowers ... the gloss of speckled feathers and washed wool with a shine like underwater velvet; warped gingham and daisy chain prints.'

This was a different kind of new romanticism, which countered the idea of power-dressing, and whose influence extended well into the next decade. Suddenly the asymmetrical cut and sensuous fabrics of Galliano were everywhere, but unlike many of his contemporaries, his look was particularly hard to translate to the ready-to-wear market; under the shock of the new silhouettes lay a luxury and attention to detail which was hard to emulate cheaply.

JOHN GALLIANO

'Consider the Lillies [sic]. Like flowers
this Collection is regular or irregular,
but always upright, flowing, sensitive...'

John Galliano promotional literature 1987

# 1988

# Jean-Paul Gaultier for Junior Gaultier

**Short black denim dress, mesh T-shirt, beret, tights and shoes**

**Chosen by Jeff Banks at *The Clothes Show***

The original fashion innovator, Jean-Paul Gaultier has had an incredible influence on the perception of style in the last 30 years, matched only by Vivienne Westwood, John Galliano and Alexander McQueen for a sheer sense of theatre. Regarded by many commentators as the *enfant terrible* of French fashion early in the decade, his collections are still amongst the most influential in Paris, initially drawing inspiration from street fashion and instinctively knowing which elements to accentuate.

With experience early in his career of working for the couture houses of Pierre Cardin and Jean Patou, his grounding in couture was impeccable. His vision was a translation into a fast-moving and dynamic world of ready-to-wear, running both his own name label and Junior Gaultier, a more affordable yet no less dynamic boutique label.

In London his shops were as memorable as his clothes, designed like Parisian boulevards with full-size replicas of circular advertising hoardings. In the late 1980s his suits were dramatically tailored, drawing inspiration from the 1930s, teaming double-breasted jackets finished with tortoise shell buttons with shorts and matelot tops. His collections mixed everything from the white, red and blue of sailors' uniforms, and the silky satin crêpe of 1940s lingerie to the intense and dense patterns of tattoo art, translated into vibrant prints.

Jeff Banks recalls of his choice: 'Jean-Paul Gaultier has always had a great sense of humour, and refined fashion by taking normally accepted standards and humorously twisting them, altering them by either fabrication or proportion. At the time all things denim were having a huge revival and what JPG did was take an ordinary denim jacket, alter the proportion of it, lengthen it, add faux sleeves and collar inserts, and turn it into an urban dress of the moment.'

Taken from the designer's first collection for Junior Gaultier, the 1988 Dress of the Year award was covered on the BBC's hugely successful *Clothes Show*, presented by Jeff Banks, Selina Scott and Caryn Franklin. It was an important indicator of the increased accessibility and popularity of catwalk fashion in the middle market.

Jeff Banks chose Jean Paul Gaultier in 1988 for his expressive sense of fun and clever reworking of the denim mini-skirt.

'His wit and humour turns fabric
and fashion on its head.'

———————

Jeff Banks

'On a catwalk scattered with
Oriental carpets with a background
painted to resemble a crumbling
façade, Ozbek paraded a virtuoso
collection that proudly displayed his
Turkish heritage. Long may he reign.'

*Cornucopia* magazine

# 1989

# Rifat Ozbek

**Evening ensemble in embroidered velvet**

**Chosen by Kathryn Samuel at *The Daily Telegraph***

Inspired by the rich and diverse palettes, textures and shapes of an Eastern bazaar, Rifat Ozbek's 1989 evening ensemble was translated for the streets of late 20th-century London, a vision of embroidered velvet and silk trimmed with fur and tiny gold trinkets.

Voted British Designer of the Year in both 1988 and 1992, Rifat Ozbek was born in Istanbul and originally came to Britain to study architecture, but transferred to fashion at St Martin's School of Art (now Central Saint Martins) in London, graduating in 1977. Via Walter Albini in Milan and high street retailer Monsoon (specialising in batiks and printed silks in the early 1980s) he opened his own company in 1984, followed by the diffusion label Future Ozbek in 1987.

Ozbek was at the forefront of fashion's new fascination with exotic world influences. By cleverly incorporating elements of ethnic costume, his collections became renowned for their originality and were amongst the most influential of the late 1980s. He reworked Islamic and native American dress, incorporating the embroidery, beading, decorated bone and appliqué into a wearable modern wardrobe. His pure white collection of 1990 was considered a masterstroke, effectively recalibrating perceptions of the Ozbek hallmark; his versatile trouser suits with decorated lapels, worn with embroidered waistcoats, were widely copied.

More recently he has been working with Armando Pollini, showing ready-to-wear in Milan, and in the field of interior design, opening Yastik, with branches in London and Turkey. He has also collaborated on several high-profile interior design projects in London.

# 1990

## Romeo Gigli

Woman's midnight blue velvet trouser suit with organza blouse

Chosen by Joan Burstein at Browns boutique

Joan Burstein, owner of Browns Boutique in London, credited Romeo Gigli with introducing a new soft and versatile shape into early 1990s fashion.

After the structured and harsh business tailoring for women in the 1980s, Romeo Gigli signalled a stylistic change of course with his soft and sensuous trouser suits for women in a range of exquisitely coloured velvets, their palette drawn from the paintings of the Italian renaissance.

The first non-fashion writer to select an award, Joan Burstein, as owner of influential boutique Browns, had a sharp eye for detail; she had, after all, been correctly spotting new fashion talent for over twenty years, and was an early supporter of John Galliano. Browns devoted an entire floor to Gigli creations, and she commented at the time: 'The exquisite colour, texture and shape of his clothes express a sensitive awareness of femininity. Just look around. He's been copied at every level. Think of wrap jersey tops, three-button jackets, narrow trousers, flat shoes – all of them from Gigli.'

Fashion journalist Dinah Hall at *The Times* agreed: 'The banishing of the shoulder pad, the softening of tailoring and the high-buttoned jacket are all credited to Romeo Gigli.' (March, 1990.)

Like Mariano Fortuny in the early 20th century, the attraction of the clothes was founded in the fabric, and from a studio above a working garage in Milan, Gigli presented the world with a comprehensive vision of a new and confident woman. Although designing since the mid-1970s, and under his own label since 1983, it was not until his 1989 'Byzantine' collection was shown in Paris that he caught the attention of the international fashion press.

However, contractual problems with business partners throughout the 1990s meant the house of Romeo Gigli was unable to expand the vision so appreciated at the time of the Dress of the Year award. It was not until 2012, and the launch of a capsule collection for the Hong Kong store Joyce, that the designer re-entered the limelight to broad applause.

'His flat-shod models pattered down the catwalk wearing the lightest of make-up and delicately unwrought chignons – the antithesis of *Working Girl*-esque bouffants and trowel-it-on face paint. His collections referenced medieval reliefs, Byzantine mosaics, Jimi Hendrix, Rastafarianism – and waifs.'

Luke Leitch, *The Daily Telegraph*, 5 September 2012

# 1991

# Karl Lagerfeld for Chanel

**Pink tweed bouclé wool jacket worn with a denim skirt, baseball cap and Chanel logo costume jewellery**

**Chosen by Elizabeth Tilberis at British *Vogue***

Since his appointment as director of design at the house of Chanel in 1983, and very much in the spirit of its founder, Karl Lagerfeld has been a master of juxtaposition, and the re-combination of existing style elements to produce something totally new. For 1991 he took a version of the classic Chanel jacket in bouclé wool and combined it with denim – normally an anathema to couture but, in this case, truly groundbreaking. It was not only a bold design statement but also an acknowledgement of the very new face of haute couture; a combination of tradition with the 'street', a luxury look worn with a baseball cap, which was to become a hallmark.

By the early 1990s, and after the conspicuous spending of the previous decade, Parisian couture was forced to reinvent itself in order to survive. Already by this time, it was the diffusion lines in ready-to-wear, perfume and accessories which enabled the great houses of Dior, Chanel and Yves Saint Laurent to subsidise their couture collection and show outfits, which in most cases retailed for many thousands of pounds.

Under the guiding hand of Lagerfeld, the distinctive Chanel logo was applied to everything from scarves to their best-selling diamond quilted handbags, and even T-shirts. In the case of the Dress of the Year ensemble, it was the multi-stranded costume necklaces that became a hallmark of Chanel catwalk shows in the early 1990s.

By incorporating elements of the great American casual revolution into his collections, he was in effect smudging the definition between couture and ready-to-wear, and expanding the audience for Chanel.

At the time of the award Liz Tilberis commented: 'Karl is fashion 1991. But I picked him not for just this year, but for the past five'. At the time his influence on couture was considerable, not only designing under his own name, but also for Chanel, Chloé and Fendi in Italy. Piracy was an increasing problem in high fashion when such large sums of money were involved. Interviewed by Avril Groom of *The Daily Telegraph* in Bath during the celebration of his award, he commented: 'Plagiarism spurs me on to change direction. The only designers that worry about it are those that are never copied.'

Karl Lagerfeld's award in 1991 was covered by *The Times*. His winning design proved to be one of the most widely copied of the decade, combining street style with a classic Chanel tweed jacket.

'This outfit is perfect for the time – a witty mix of high fashion and street cred. Seeing it on the catwalk was a real goosebumps moment, although a lot of people didn't like it at the time. Six months later it's being copied at every level of the market.'

Elizabeth Tilberis

# 1992

## Ralph Lauren

Woman's black and white pinstripe trouser suit
and shirt

Chosen by Liz Smith at *The Times*

'It's sexy, it's sharp. This sort
of tailoring gives a woman
a feeling of freedom and
a sense of her own style.
It's also where I started in
the business, doing pure
menswear for women.'

Ralph Lauren

The original lifestyle label, Ralph Lauren was one of
the most successful and influential American brands
of the 1980s and 1990s. It sold aspirational clothes,
interiors and perfumes, and spearheaded a widely
copied style of advertising, both on screen and
billboards, that was soon to become the norm.

1992 saw the 25th anniversary of Ralph Lauren in
business, and for a designer who had begun as a
salesman for Brooks Brothers his list of 'firsts' was
extensive. He was the original pioneer of menswear
for women, basing successive collections on the
premise that fashion-conscious women had been
stealing clothes from their partners' wardrobes for
years. The tuxedo, the blazer and the polo shirt were
all reworked to some effect, and from the late 1970s
Ralph Lauren became associated with a particular
kind of all-American 'preppy' style.

Liz Smith commented: 'Of all American designer labels
his is unquestionably the most recognised. Lauren
opened up the idea of 'real' clothes and selling them
against an idealised backdrop of New England
firesides or Long Island beach houses, all lovingly
created in his Madison Avenue or Bond Street shops
and in his advertising campaigns.'

By restyling perennial favourites he was able to
breathe new life into a variety of looks, ironically selling
formal tailoring in London – cricket whites and striped
silk ties – just yards away from Savile Row and the
clubs of St James's, the style of which he was choosing
to emulate. By combining this with the enormous
popularity for his 'Polo' casual clothes and fragrances
he was able to deformalise elements from established
dress by combining them with denim, chinos and
T-shirts for men, women and, latterly, children.

Some fashion commentators at the time of the award
wondered just how many women would wear a suit
complete with shirt and tie as presented on the
catwalk but, ever a master of supplying a demand,
Ralph Lauren also showed the suit with bare
décolletage for evening, or with a polo neck for day.

# 1993

## Donna Karan

Purple wool and stretch velvet dress, hat and boots

Chosen by Glenda Bailey at *Marie Claire*

'I feel very strongly about dresses on every level – a dress feels like underpinning.'

Donna Karan

After the structured and harsh business tailoring for women in the 1980s, Romeo Gigli signalled a stylistic change of course with his soft and sensuous trouser suits for women in a range of exquisitely coloured velvets, their palette drawn from the paintings of the Italian renaissance.

The first non-fashion writer to select an award, Joan Burstein, as owner of influential boutique Browns, had a sharp eye for detail; she had, after all, been correctly spotting new fashion talent for over twenty years, and was an early supporter of John Galliano. Browns devoted an entire floor to Gigli creations, and she commented at the time: 'The exquisite colour, texture and shape of his clothes express a sensitive awareness of femininity. Just look around. He's been copied at every level. Think of wrap jersey tops, three-button jackets, narrow trousers, flat shoes – all of them from Gigli.'

Fashion journalist Dinah Hall at *The Times* agreed: 'The banishing of the shoulder pad, the softening of tailoring and the high-buttoned jacket are all credited to Romeo Gigli.' (March, 1990)

Like Mariano Fortuny in the early 20th century, the attraction of the clothes was founded in the fabric, and from a studio above a working garage in Milan, Gigli presented the world with a comprehensive vision of a new and confident woman. Although designing since the mid-1970s, and under his own label since 1983, it was not until his 1989 'Byzantine' collection was shown in Paris that he caught the attention of the international fashion press.

However, contractual problems with business partners throughout the 1990s meant the house of Romeo Gigli was unable to expand the vision so appreciated at the time of the Dress of the Year award. It was not until 2012, and the launch of a capsule collection for the Hong Kong store Joyce, that the designer re-entered the limelight to broad applause.

# 1993

## Donna Karan

Purple wool and stretch velvet dress, hat and boots

Chosen by Glenda Bailey at *Marie Claire*

One of a trio of highly influential American designers in the 1980s and 1990s, Donna Karan will always be associated with the city of New York. Along with Calvin Klein and Ralph Lauren, she perfected the casual wardrobe – ironically as coolly coordinated as any formal one – for her clients who wanted clothes that could translate effortlessly from day to night and back again.

Donna Karan New York and her diffusion line, DKNY, epitomise the urban chic of the city, and, like her fellow American designers, she created a global business on the back of effective and original advertising campaigns.

In a career that began with designer Anne Klein in 1967, it was not until 1985 that Donna Karan formed her own label, specifically to translate her own taste in fashion into her collections, with practicality and realistic body shapes in mind. It was a bold and refreshingly new approach to fashion at a time when subtlety of design was far from the norm.

Donna Karan's clothes reflected her lifestyle, balancing the needs for a business wardrobe, coordinated casuals and evening wear, which translated between city and upstate, day and evening. With her use of lycra, she specifically set out to design for women without a perfect shape. One of her most popular innovations was the 'body', which could be worn under a jacket and, when combined with a wrap skirt or structured tailoring, became the modern foundation garment of choice.

Her purple wool and stretch velvet dress of 1993 incorporates the hallmark 'body'; it is formal enough for evening, and easily dressed up or down. The use of stretch velvet – a favourite for evening wear in the early 1990s – gives the dress an added subtle luxury.

Worn with statement jewellery, the ensemble summarises much of the Donna Karan look – strong, simple shapes; fluid, draped and wrapped fabrics. In effect, a new 'casual formality' designed to be worn to the office, then on into the evening.

# 1994

## John Galliano

Bias cut full length black silk evening dress

Chosen by Meredith Etherington-Smith at
*Harpers & Queen*

Just a year before joining Givenchy as the first British designer to be appointed head of a Parisian couture house, John Galliano was at the height of his powers, his evident genius for showmanship and innovation becoming increasingly apparent.

However, his career since graduating from Central Saint Martins in 1984 had not been an easy one; as with many other designers at the time, finding a way to convert original ideas into a profitable business remained elusive. Galliano designs were understandably hard to translate into the mass-market, and many relied on the intricate and subtle cutting more often associated with a couture atelier. A further Designer of the Year Award in 1994 cemented his place as the rising star of not just British, but international fashion; he was ultimately to be rewarded with a position as head of design at Christian Dior in 1996, after just two years at Givenchy.

Meredith Etherington-Smith's choice of his full-length black silk evening dress offers the definitive Galliano masterclass in bias cutting. Exploiting his genius for accentuation, he lengthened and exaggerated the classic 1930s evening dress to offer a dramatic and theatrical garment which, ironically given its impracticality, became increasingly influential in mainstream design. Discarding the length and luxury, the Galliano bias cut evening dress became the prototype for high street copies, just as couture originals have always been.

Tempted to Paris from London, he followed a well-worn path, as showing couture in London still played second fiddle to Paris, Milan and New York. There his collections blossomed into full-blown, historically inspired extravaganzas which set a new standard in the presentation of couture shows, noted for their originality and excess. He raided the Dior archive to launch a new 'New Look' and, magpie-like, assembled collections inspired by boudoir dolls, pirates and Marie Antoinette.

If modern couture was about gaining headline space, on the back of which diffusion lines could be sold, Galliano without doubt set the pace for the remainder of the decade.

'Dressing up.
People just don't do it anymore.
We have to change that.'

John Galliano

# 1995

# Catherine Rayner and Tom Gilbey

Beaded ivory silk satin wedding dress by Catherine Rayner worn with duchesse satin mules by Emma Hope. Ivory silk damask Nehru jacket, wool trousers and embroidered waistcoat by Tom Gilbey

Chosen by Sandra Boler at *Brides* magazine

Catherine Rayner's opulent wedding dress is one of only two to feature in the Dress of the Year awards since 1963, modelled here by Rachel de Thame with menswear by Tom Gilbey.

Perhaps surprisingly for clothing with such a specific function, the wedding dress is a fascinating barometer of taste at any given time. Chosen just twice as Dress of The Year, in 1975 and 1995, both examples can trace their design origins back to historical formal dress. In the case of Gina Fratini it was the Victorian period; with Catherine Rayner, it is the slightly plainer look of the early 20th century.

What also links them is the romantic vision of a traditional wedding, but unlike the majority of bridal dresses up to the 1970s, there is no broad reflection of the prevalent styles in evening wear at the time. Instead, there is the separate development of a fashion reserved especially for the great day, a one-off 'dressing-up box', containing different looks inspired by any point from the 18th to the 20th century.

Catherine Rayner, a bridal designer of some repute in the mid-1990s, created a dress in heavy white duchesse satin, the neckline decorated with ribbon, bows and tiny pearl beads, the skirts gathered in a modern version of a bustle to the rear. With satin-covered mules by Emma Hope (the shoes of choice for any 1990s bride), the fantasy was complete, and could easily be replicated by the readers of *Brides* magazine via the designer's boutique, or from select London department stores like Dickins & Jones.

Tom Gilbey's ivory brocade Nehru jacket tackled the perennial problem of updating the groom in a way that would match the bride. Its simple shape executed in a luxurious fabric harks back to the menswear revolution of London in the late 1960s, when the designer launched his notable career, selling a new brand of Savile Row tailored sophistication alongside the likes of Michael Fish, Blades and Tommy Nutter. Still successfully designing in the 1990s, he specialised in just this brand of understated elegance, together with sought-after, bespoke hand-painted waistcoats.

'A perfect reflection of the current trend of nostalgia and period costume.'

Sandra Boler

FUJI RHP

RHP ▷ 16

# Alexander McQueen and Paul Smith

Red and black brocade tunic with slashed detail worn with red 'bumster' slim-cut trousers by Alexander McQueen. Brilliant blue two-piece suit and shirt by Paul Smith

---

Chosen by Tamsin Blanchard at *The Independent*

Already labelled the new *enfant terrible* of British fashion, Alexander McQueen was about to embark on a brief but incredibly influential career in fashion when his controversial 'bumster' trousers and slashed brocade jacket were selected by Tamsin Blanchard. The outfit, which featured the model's 'rear cleavage' (as the Fashion Museum press release termed it), formed part of the designer's notorious and seminal Spring/Summer 1996 collection, 'Hunger'. The revealing red trousers contrast with an opulent floral brocade top in rich metallic colours, with hanging sleeves lined in red.

Tamsin Blanchard commented: 'Alexander McQueen has been one of the best ambassadors for British fashion since John Galliano. His clothes sum up a certain attitude and spirit that will, in hindsight, be one of the strongest images of cutting-edge style in the mid-nineties. I chose his brocade tunic and bumster trousers because they are both intricately tailored and finished in fine couture brocade, as well as being challenging and intriguing. He has also secured his place in the fashion history books with his recent appointment as successor to Galliano at the House of Givenchy.' (Tamsin Blanchard to the Fashion Museum, Bath, 1996.)

The designer was interviewed by *Harpers & Queen* in August 1996, shortly after his new appointment was announced, and responded to accusations that, although provocative, his collection was uncommercial: 'Critics complained that there was nothing to buy, as if I'm that stupid that I would do something completely unwearable by accident. It was my last collection on the dole. I knew it was my chance to say what I wanted without having to sell.'

Paul Smith, by contrast, had been creating definitive menswear for his boutiques since 1970. His clothes combined hallmark features of cut and quality with original colours, textures and tailoring – his electric blue wool and rayon two-buttoned suit was a classic shape in a high-tech and very contemporary fabric. Tamsin Blanchard recalled, 'Paul Smith's clothes are a fine balance between what is shown in style magazines and what men really wear. He has become a British institution with a business that influences the way men dress from Nottingham to Nagasaki. I felt that it was important to choose menswear, because men have undergone a revolution in the past few years, in their attitudes towards the way they dress and their increased awareness of fashion, labels and clothes shopping.'

Opposite page
Jimmy Pursey of Sham 69 models Paul Smith, with Tizer Bailey in Alexander McQueen's slashed brocade jacket and 'bumster' trousers.

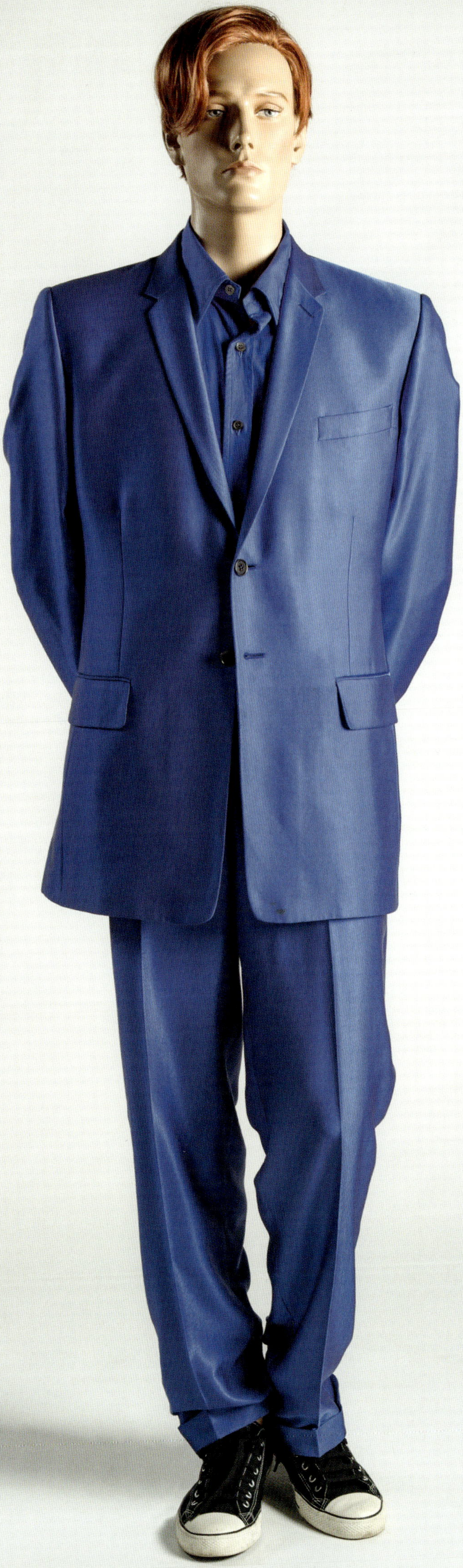

Alexander McQueen's 'bumster' trousers challenged
taste and caused a sensation, but less severe
versions were widely copied by high street retailers.
Alexander McQueen

'Not since McQueen's mentor Yves Saint Laurent was appointed designer at Christian Dior at the tender age of 21, has one designer achieved so much in so short a time.'

Tamsin Blanchard

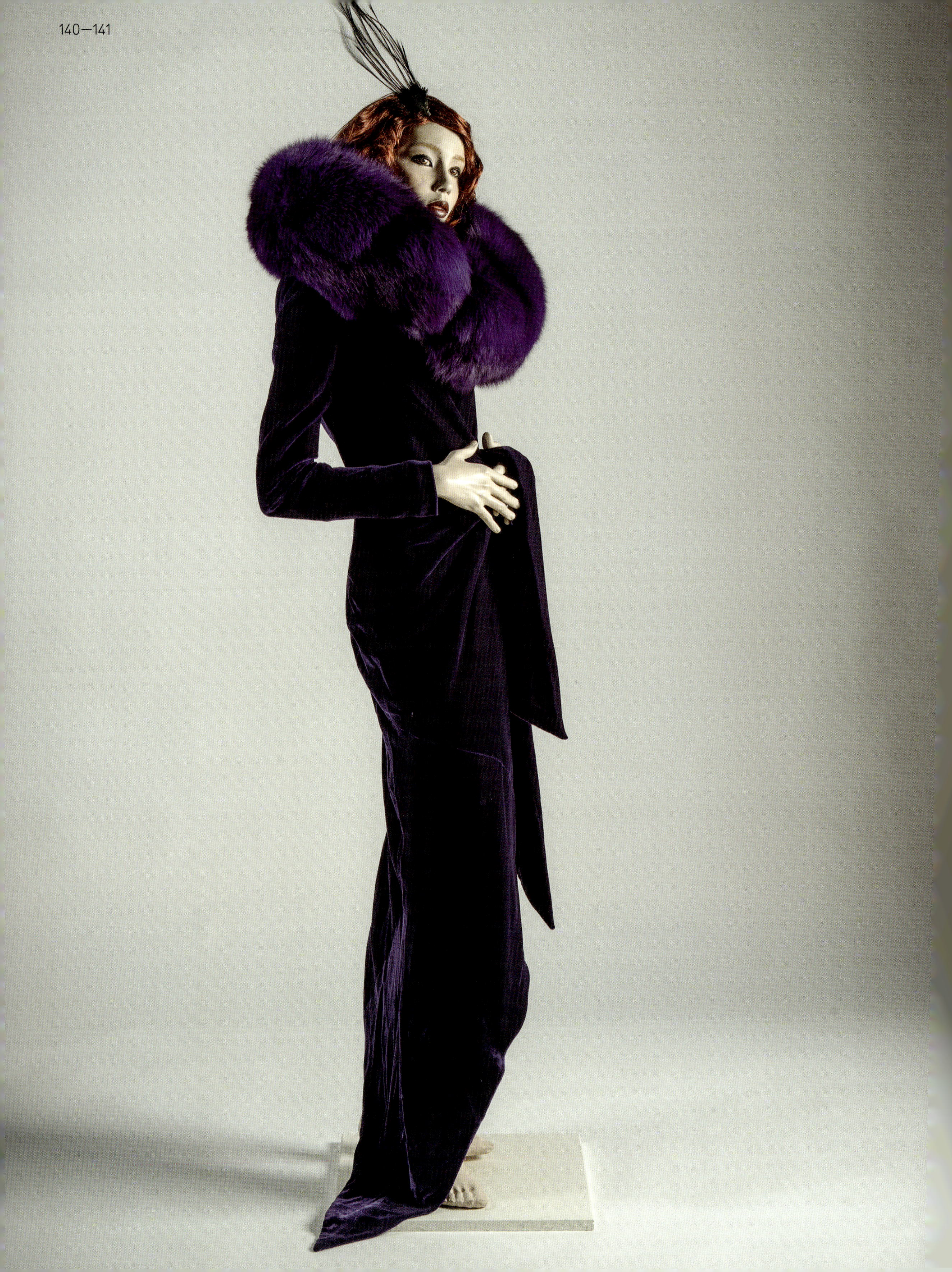

# 1997

## Hussein Chalayan, Julien Macdonald, Lainey Keogh, Deborah Milner, Philip Treacy, Mr Pearl and Shaun Leane

Purple evening dress with sunburst bead embroidery by Hussein Chalayan. Gold knitted rayon and horsehair 'mermaid' dress by Julien MacDonald. Beaded knitted evening dress and coat by Lainey Keogh. Purple velvet evening coat with fur collar by Deborah Milner. Black sculpted 'bonnet' by Philip Treacy. Black corset by Mr Pearl. Silver mouthpiece by Shaun Leane

**Chosen by Isabella Blow at *The Sunday Times***

With a reputation for spotting talent early (including Philip Treacy, Alexander McQueen and Sophie Dahl) and a sense of personal style as distinctive as anything at the catwalk shows she attended, it is perhaps not surprising that Isabella Blow felt inspired to select a cornucopia of seven fashionable pieces in 1997. All were in some way interconnected. Her selection combines craft, millinery, jewellery, dressmaking and corsetry to provide a fascinating snap-shot of a particular variety of high fashion, and again serves to emphasise her own risk-taking nature in matters of taste.

Credited with his discovery, a hat by Philip Treacy was her hallmark; in this case it was an oversized bonnet, a sinuous curve of black straw finished with blood-red feathers, as dramatic as anything conceived by Cecil Beaton for *My Fair Lady*. On the subject of her penchant for a Treacy hat at all times, she commented to *The Guardian*, 'I don't use a hat as a prop, I use it as part of me. If I am feeling really low I go and see Philip, cover my face and feel fantastic.' (*The Guardian*, 'Blow by Blow', 23 June 2002.)

Isabella Blow's personal style marked her out as one of the most memorable figures in the fashion world. For 1997 she chose seven separate designs, here seen with Philip Treacy's black straw bonnet and Shaun Leane's silver mouthpiece.

With a surrealist tint running through her choices, a rayon and horsehair knitted dress from celebrity favourite Julien Macdonald reveals almost as much as it conceals, and combines the classic shape of an occasion gown with an innovative and unusual material. Similarly, a beaded and knitted evening dress by Irish designer Lainey Keogh, Hussein Chalayan's simple aubergine shift dress with L-shaped beading from his 'Scent of Tempests' Autumn/Winter 1997 collection, and a purple velvet evening coat by Deborah Milner all combine luxury, texture and craft in a modern version of the glittering tasselled and beaded evening dresses and coats of the 1920s. Milner in particular was a great favourite. Once described in a Fashion Museum press release as 'London's best-kept secret for extraordinarily beautiful designs', she too had collaborated with both Phillip Treacy and Alexander McQueen on a number of occasions.

Mark Pullin, aka Mr Pearl, brought the art of the corset to a new generation of wearers, creating exclusive designs for Jean Paul Gaultier, Thierry Mugler and Alexander McQueen, amongst a host of other couture houses. Sporting an 18-inch waist himself, at the time of the award he operated a corset shop in London where every piece was made by hand to traditional techniques. With a renewed interest in burlesque, wearers such as Dita Von Teese and Sophie Dahl still act as Mr Pearl's very own glamorous calling cards.

For over a decade Shaun Leane provided the dramatic, mannerist jewellery and body sculpture to accompany the clothes of Alexander McQueen, an indication of the innovation and strength of design with which he built his substantial following. First collaborating on McQueen's 1995 'Hunger' collection, it was his sometimes disturbing vision which managed to pace the inspired and innovative clothes he produced for Givenchy, and later under the Alexander McQueen label.

In a reflection of how the process of jewellery and catwalk fashion design are mirrored, he too has achieved enormous success retailing more commercial versions of his work, using statement pieces such as his 1996 silver mouthpiece 'Repression' (shown in the McQueen Autumn/Winter collection of 1997) just as fashion designers use their couture shows – as theatrical 'tasters' for the clothes and accessories retailed in boutiques and smart department stores worldwide.

# 1998

## Sonia Rykiel and Chris Bailey

Sonia Rykiel skilfully combined the influence of street fashion with her hallmark Parisian luxury in her winning ensemble for Dress of the Year in 1998.
Sonia Rykiel

**ELLEfashion**

### THE LOOKS OF THE YEAR

We've been flooded with fabulous design, but ELLE's Iain R Webb had the unenviable task of choosing the 1998 Dress of the Year

Sonia Rykiel is still inspired by the street, even though her designs are the ultimate in French sophistication

'I wanted to choose outfits that show that fashion now takes its influence from the streets. The combat jacket and parka embody 'utility chic' which is everywhere on the international catwalk.'

Iain R Webb

Woman's black knitted sweater worn with combat trousers and pink marabou stole by Sonia Rykiel. Man's silver-grey suit, white T-shirt and knee-length puffa jacket by Chris Bailey

Chosen by Iain R Webb at *Elle* magazine

Iain R Webb's approach to making his choice for 1998 was simple and definite: 'I wanted to choose something which wasn't simply a showstopper – the kind of thing that makes the front page of a newspaper but never exists beyond the catwalk.'

From Sonia Rykiel, a designer who had been working and selling in Paris since 1968, came black knitted combat trousers teamed with a hallmark rhinestone-studded sweater, a pink marabou feather boa adding a touch of glamour. At the time, Iain R Webb told his readers at *Elle*, 'Rykiel is still inspired by the street, even though her designs are the ultimate in French sophistication'.

It was this effortless chic which had meant that as a designer she attracted a loyal and extensive following, particularly for her elegant knitwear: layered, figure-hugging and fluid elements combined in equal measure, more often than not in her signature palette of neutrals, greys and blues.

Jigsaw was founded in 1972 by John and Belle Robinson to sell and manufacture high-quality womenswear. In 1994 Chris Bailey launched their menswear range, specifically to fill a gap in the market which existed between the high street retailers and the international brands, providing high fashion for men at the upper end of mainstream prices; he bought the business outright in 1998.

His sleek, grey single-breasted suit is simple and sophisticated; teamed with a quilted parka, the look is edgier, priced well below Helmut Lang, Gaultier or Prada but still the perfect partner for Sonia Rykiel's vision of luxury urban cool.

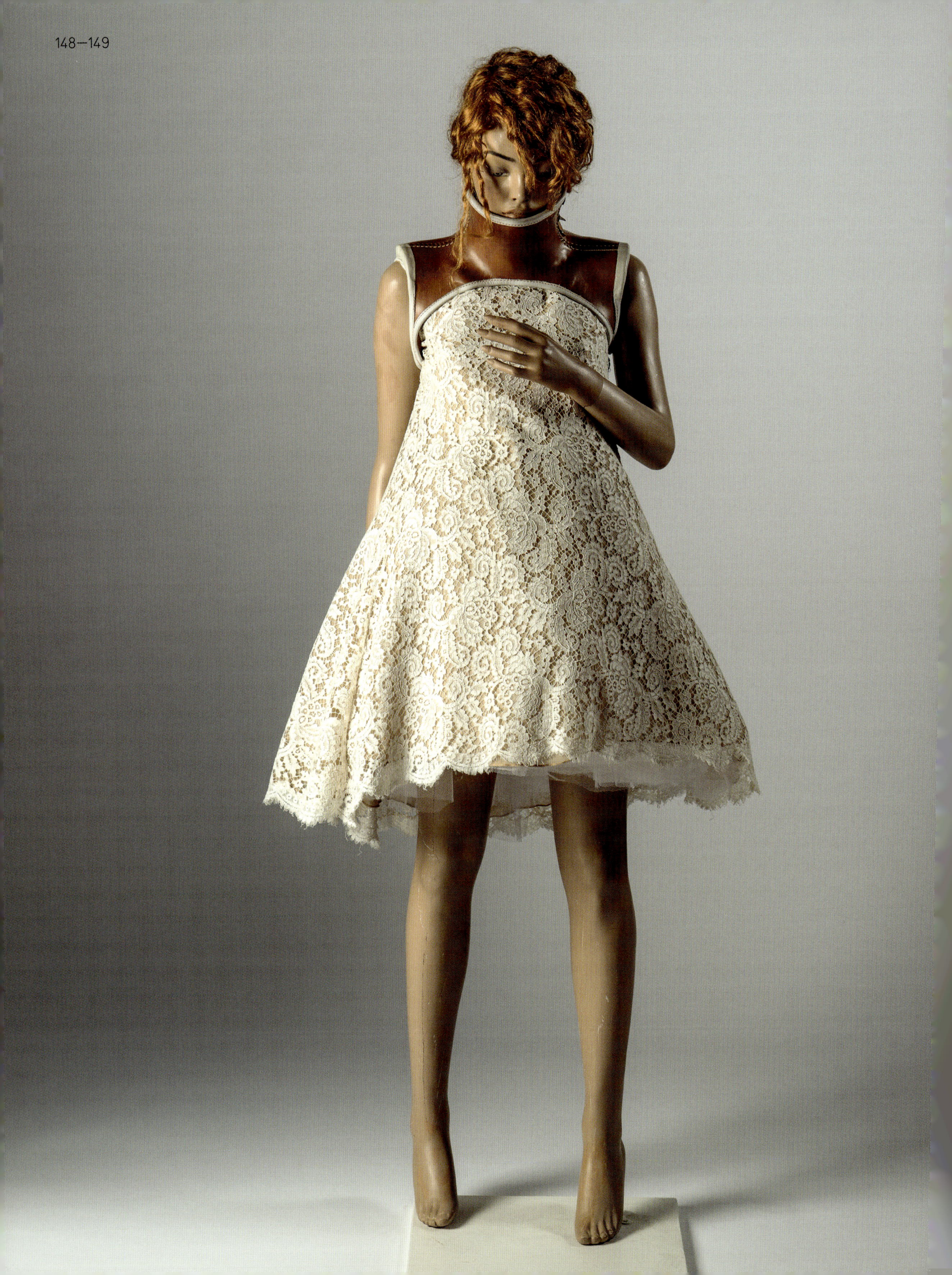

# 1999

## Alexander McQueen

**Cream lace dress with brown leather collar and sandals**

**Chosen by Susannah Frankel at *The Independent***

Closing the 20th century: a definitive ensemble by Alexander McQueen. Taken from his Spring/Summer 1999 collection, the short cream lace tapering dress with graduated hem, worn over a caramel silk slip and net underskirts, is a structured, sculptural confection, almost baroque in its inspiration. Finished with a brown moulded leather collar resembling a neck-brace, and together with high-heeled sandals in cream and brown leather, the ensemble is both feminine and disturbing; the hallmarks of McQueen.

Susannah Frankel commented at the time: 'His Spring/Summer 1999 collection, in particular, was his finest to date, showing the designer in softer and more romantic mood than he has been. Despite the fact that this was his last collection for the current millennium, rather than taking a predictable space age/futuristic route, the designer harked back to the Arts and Crafts movement and sent out wooden skirts, raffia trouser suits and dresses made out of crystal-embellished mesh. Less extreme perhaps, but undoubtedly the sweetest garment in the collection was this little bell-shaped lace dress. McQueen being McQueen, any sugary overtones are undercut by the paradoxically severe and constricting collar in moulded leather that finishes the piece.'

At a time when the majority of fashion designers were looking to the future for inspiration, McQueen's masterstroke was to reference the end of the previous century. One of the strongest themes of the collection was the combination of delicate and feminine laces in beige and nude tones with leather waistcoats, halters and collars, emphasising soft and harsh materials and spurring a rush for lace on the High Street.

The theme of disability appeared with the neck-brace, albeit a bespoke creation in fine leather, and with the inclusion of Paralympic athlete Aimee Mullins as a catwalk model. For her, McQueen created a bespoke pair of carved prosthetic legs, worn with a tiered lace skirt and similar leather brace and bodice. In 2011 she recalled wearing the ensemble for the Costume Institute's retrospective exhibition: 'His clothes have always been very sensuous ... so hard and strict and unrelenting ... and then this incredibly romantic swishing of the raffia.'

'Alexander McQueen is the most exciting British fashion designer working at the close of the 20th century. His work is challenging, pushing at the boundaries of what is and isn't acceptable in clothing, while always demonstrating a clear commercial sense.'

Susannah Frankel

# 2000

# Donatella Versace for Versace

**Bamboo print silk chiffon evening dress worn with jewelled mules**

**Chosen by Lisa Armstrong at *The Times***

As the celebrities' favourite designer, Donatella Versace's forte remains the red carpet dress. At a time of intense competition for coverage in the host of newly launched fashion and gossip magazines, her Spring/Summer 2000 collection bamboo print chiffon evening dress was in fact little more than a robe. Caught and barely closed at the front with a jewelled clasp, it guaranteed attention, retailing at just over £5,000.

What started as a beach dress, modelled by Amber Valletta in the Versace catwalk show with a range of matching swimwear, quickly began to snowball in popularity. First it was worn by the designer herself to the Costume Institute Gala in December 1999; next, in January 2000, came Geri Halliwell at the NRJ Music awards. In February, Jennifer Lopez stepped out at the Oscars and her picture was everywhere, exploiting the cut of the silk chiffon gown to its limits. Suddenly fashion was all about celebrity endorsement. MTV, award ceremonies and Hollywood became increasingly important in the promotion of designers' profiles, with couture houses thinking nothing of employing full-time ambassadors to Los Angeles to convince celebrities to wear their creations to the Oscars.

Lisa Armstrong, then fashion editor at *The Times*, noticed that this was a dress that represented an era. 'The instant I saw JLo at the Oscars in this dress, I thought, there's a moment. The trend throughout the Noughties was for ever lighter, skimpier clothes – and a lot of tit tape. What these clothes lacked in mystique, they more than made up for in ingenuity. How did they stay up? How did the designer do that? How many hours has that celebrity put in at the gym/with the surgeon? How far down this line are these actresses and musicians prepared to go before it backfires – think what happened to Cher's acting career after she wore transparent Bob Mackie to the Oscars in the '80s. These were the questions you found yourself constantly asking at the time. As a piece of fashion history, I think this dress is perfect – it brings it all back and I must say, Donatella was incredibly generous and easy to deal with over it. One phone call and the dress was on a plane.'

About as revealing as any dress could get, Jennifer Lopez wore Versace's printed chiffon gown to the Oscars in 2000, capturing the front page across the globe.
Getty Images

'It just summed up everything that was going on at the time: the obsession with baring as much as you possibly could on the red carpet to get headlines – and the subsequent requirement for a perfect, air-brushed body.'

Lisa Armstrong 2013

Chris Moore/Catwalking

# Tom Ford for Yves Saint Laurent

'Peasant' ensemble of gauze top and velvet satin skirt, with boots and velvet scarf

Chosen by Alexandra Shulman at British *Vogue*

Already credited with revitalising the venerable Italian fashion house of Gucci in the 1990s, Tom Ford was also installed as creative director of Yves Saint Laurent Rive Gauche in 2000, shortly before Saint Laurent's retirement. Like Gucci, the Rive Gauche label had an illustrious past and was at its most fashionable in the mid to late 1970s. Tom Ford's solution in both cases was to inject a sensuous glamour, Hollywood-style, and match it with exquisitely shot advertising campaigns by Mario Testino. His hallmarks were exquisite and daringly lean tailoring, black and purple silks and satin, low-buttoned, crisp white cotton shirts, and an inherent understanding of the 'less is more' ethos – simple, strong design and tightly coherent, wearable clothes.

In his Autumn/Winter 2001 collection he drew inspiration from the gypsy style so beloved by Saint Laurent, his black satin skirt and off-the-shoulder 'peasant' top woven with feathers and velvet, worn with a panné velvet scarf and black gladiator-style leather boots.

Creating a mixture of bohemian and cosmopolitan chic, he said of the collection, 'There are a lot of references to Mr Saint Laurent's work: the smocks, the gypsies, but I added my own personal touch. Nobody needs to remake what Mr Saint Laurent has already done. I spent quite a lot of time in the archives, I simply wanted to absorb the past and then bring in my own ideas. The collection was really about French bohemian chic. Some of my favourite pieces are the off-the-shoulder tops, leaving the shoulders naked ... all the handwork is a slight bohemian look. I wanted it to look real and sensual.'

Tom Ford's genius did not come cheaply, however, with this luxury ready-to-wear ensemble retailing at over £6,000.

'This outfit epitomises an incredibly influential collection. It combines a soft romanticism with the strength and modernity of that Autumn 2001 season in its tough leather boots, its overall blackness. Tom Ford was one of the first designers to tap into the haute-folk vein, a movement that is now hugely popular.'

Alexandra Shulman

# 2002

## Junya Watanabe

Patchwork knit and jersey dress worn with distressed cow-hide shoes by Junya Watanabe

Chosen by at Hilary Alexander at *The Daily Telegraph*

Under the watchful eye of Comme des Garçons founder Rei Kawakubo, Junya Watanabe continued what the label had started in the 1980s by producing challenging, deconstructed clothes for a new audience. At Comme des Garçons menswear he learnt to take nothing for granted; the accepted tradition of form and beauty did not apply in this case, and there were very often no rules applied to the technically outstanding and original placing and exposure of the construction techniques which made up any garment.

His long black patchwork dress teamed with distressed brown cowhide brogues, from the Autumn/Winter 2002 collection, is constructed from misshapen and variously textured sections of knit, weave, and jersey, and closes with laces to the rear. An exercise in deconstruction, the dress is, however, surprisingly elegant, combining elements of experimentation with a vaguely bohemian feel.

Watanabe's clothes embrace new textile technology and construction techniques with vigour, reflected in the way his catwalk shows leave large gaps between models, so that the complexity of each design can be appreciated. His signature is the unexpected; mis-matched zips; random, gathered pleating and smocking; the exaggeration of scale of elements within a garment; even removing the backs of his clothes completely to expose a second, very different, look beneath.

Not necessarily designed to shock, rather to intrigue, his collections are united by a different experiment each season: in 1995 he combined black wool and leather, and heavily tattooed models; in 1997 it was cut-away kimono-inspired florals; in 1999 it was the layered and draped fabrics associated with the sari.

Watanabe's Autumn/Winter 2002 collection was held in a dimly-lit former music hall in Paris and combined elegant dresses in a palette of greys and blacks, but in each case either distressed or deconstructed. Sarah Mower attended the show and observed, 'he's a sensitive soul, more prone to bursts of cheerfulness than angst, and the collection came across as delicate and melancholy rather than doom-laden'.

'Watanabe's collection was composed almost entirely of dusty-grey '30s-styled dresses in satin, cotton and velvet, often bias cut and/or backless, and always in an artful state of distress. Hems were riddled with holes, as though the grey-lipsticked wearers had walked away from some disaster in their sturdy leather biker boots and crooked, incinerated Edwardian hats.'

Sarah Mower, *style.com,* March 2002

Chris Moore/Catwalking

# Marni

Colourful printed floral cotton ensemble with
jewellery-encrusted shoulder bag

Chosen by Lucinda Chambers at British *Vogue*

'This collection seemed really fresh and easy, almost spontaneous, as if nothing had been particularly thought out and was layered together in a haphazard way. It seemed so effortless. That is perhaps Marni's greatest strength: one season never negates the other, it always feels like an evolution.'

Lucinda Chambers

Bringing together her pretty floral prints, bohemian, gypsy and folk trends, designer Consuelo Castiglioni's Spring/Summer 2003 ensemble is relaxed and casual – a master-class in the 'uncoordinated coordination' for which Marni has become renowned. A great hit with the fashion-buying public, this easy-to-wear 'rock chick' chic was prettiness with an edge, personified by actresses like Sienna Miller, whose personal style was followed closely by the fashion media at the time.

Lucinda Chambers said of the designer, 'I think that this collection brought together everything that Marni loves, the mix of the print and texture, flowers and stripes, fur and leather. Marni doesn't change the goal posts each season. People who love Marni really like the feeling that if they bought something ten years ago it would still be relevant in their wardrobe today. If you fall in love with the print or the shape, you can still wear it with the current collection. In that way it becomes emotive, not wanting to be on a trend, but imagining yourself at seventy still wearing and enjoying it.'

The Marni look also encompassed skilful juxtaposition, combining broderie anglaise chemise tops with fur; the shortest of shorts with 1940s feminine floral print chiffon blouses; slouchy shift tea dresses with neat short blazers; even cabbage rose print cotton trousers for men. The 'It' bag was another phenomenon of the period, where one or two designs would become the 'must-have' accessory that season, spurred on by coverage in the media. Marni's version for 2003 was a brown leather outsize shoulder bag, the strap covered with a mass of trinkets, from diamante brooches to fine chains and coloured, stone-set pendants.

By combining and coordinating cleverly, Castiglioni also acknowledged the popularity of vintage clothes and textiles, with increasing numbers of designers and retailers referencing exactly the type of floral prints seen in the 2003 Dress of the Year.

On the UK high street, retailers including Topshop and Oasis used original 'document' prints from vintage garments sourced from antiques markets and dealers, reproducing them in ranges of easily coordinated clothes, and adding a nostalgic accent to their modern collections.

# 2004

# Tom Ford for Yves Saint Laurent

**Evening dress in Chinese dragon print silk**

*Chosen by at Sarajane Hoare at Vanity Fair*

Arguably producing some of the most elegant and dramatic designs of his career, Tom Ford's Autumn/ Winter 2004 collection for Rive Gauche was ironically to be his last for the fashion house before he embarked on a successful solo career.

Shortly before retiring in 2002, Yves Saint Laurent had closed his couture label, leaving Tom Ford as head of Rive Gauche under the ownership of Gucci Group. There he joined a select group of talented designers who had revitalised venerable names, beginning with Saint Laurent himself at Christian Dior in the late 1950s, and John Galliano in the 1990s, along with Karl Lagerfeld at Chanel, Stella McCartney at Chloé and Alexander McQueen at Givenchy.

Drawing inspiration from the palette of Oriental lacquers and referencing Saint Laurent's seminal 1977 Chinese collection, he combined 'pagoda' shoulders with exquisite printed silks, hourglass shapes incorporating finely tailored bustiers, bias cutting, and fishtail skirts. Also appearing were the Tom Ford keynote satins in midnight blue and jet black, echoing the sensuous sophistication of the Dress of the Year 2001.

Carrying the theme through the majority of the collection, what appears on printed silk in the Dress of the Year 2004 was repeated in beading on a similar design, the body of the dress composed of glittering black sequins. This was a final curtain call, all about luxury and texture. It combined the opulence of silk brocade trimmed with fur, faux-leopardskin coats over banded satin and crêpe-de-chine cheongsam dresses, and satin-lapelled tuxedos for women – the ultimate nod to Saint Laurent's famous 'Le Smoking' of 1966.

His designs proved a particular success on the red carpet in 2004, with Nicole Kidman wearing the dress to the Tony Awards in June. Moreover, via a provocative nude advertising campaign featuring Sophie Dahl, he applied the same skill of targeted promotion to the Rive Gauche perfume 'Opium'.

Chris Moore/Catwalking

'The dress epitomises Tom Ford's ability to dip into the Yves Saint Laurent archive, in this case YSL's famous Chinese collection, and to come up with something completely original and completely right for 2004.'

Sarajane Hoare

# 2005

# Alber Elbaz for Lanvin/Thom Browne

**Blue silk faille dress with full skirt by Albar Elbaz.
Two-piece man's suit by Thom Browne**

**Chosen by Charlie Porter at *The Guardian/GQ***

Lanvin, one of the oldest and certainly one of the most venerated names in French couture, had been out of the fashion spotlight since its signature bold prints of the early 1970s. Desperately in need of rejuvenation, and after a series of corporate owners in the intervening period, the brand was back in private hands by the time Alber Elbaz was appointed artistic director in 2001.

His earlier experience designing at Guy Laroche and Yves Saint Laurent quickly translated into critical acclaim for the refreshed Lanvin label, his Spring/Summer 2005 collection being particularly successful. It retraced the steps of Jeanne Lanvin and centred on silk faille and gazar, this time washed and more supple to reduce rigidity.

Alongside drop-waisted panier dresses (which harked backed to Lanvin's early 1920s heyday, and mirror an original already in the Fashion Museum collection) he showed outsize trench coats with bold tied belts, neatly tailored short wiggle dresses, 'skater skirts' teamed with tailored blazer jackets, short Grecian-inspired tunic dresses, and tiered peasant skirts with pretty cardigans. All were in neutrals or soft tones of pink, blue and yellow.

For New York-based tailor Thom Browne, suits are all about proportion. His 2005 Edwardian-inspired two-piece with braid-trimmed details adjusts this. The trousers, worn high up on the waist, emphasise a shorter leg; the jacket, snug and fitted, challenges the norm and injects a risqué element into a bastion of tradition. He commented, 'I've always been turned off by suits where the jacket was too much a part of it, as opposed to the jacket and trousers being one. For me, this jacket and trousers work perfectly together. There's nothing extraneous about it.' (Fashion Museum press release, 2005.)

Not since the Italian suits of the early 1960s had men's tailoring been quite so lean or quite so sharp, designed to be worn complete, or with the new skinny jeans.

*The Guardian 'Weekend'*
magazine, 3 December 2005,
photographer Rolph Gobits

Stylebistro.com / Imaxtree

'For me the dress is like a new uniform. There's something very easy about it, you put it on then you don't have to think about it. As a fashion designer, you either create for a fashion show or you create fashion for life. You either do pieces that work with women, or you steal their faces. What you should see is the face and not the dress. The dress should disappear.'

Alber Elbaz, *The Guardian*, 3 December 2005

# Prada

Woman's olive green coat with fur patch pockets

Chosen by Sarah Mower, fashion journalist

'This outfit sums up the subversive twist Prada puts into her work at its best. She is, of course, a high fashion designer who sells her work at the highest prices, but she still managed to make the fur patch pockets on this parka look somehow feral and a bit disturbing.'

Sara Mower

Chris Moore/Catwalking

Founded in 1913 and originally selling leather goods, Prada was revitalised by the arrival of Miuccia Prada in 1978. She has cautiously expanded the brand and now, after adding clothes to the label's portfolio, sells across the globe. Her hallmarks are a minimalist and distinctively Italian chic, epitomised throughout the 1990s by a uniform of black, teamed with the obligatory Prada bag displaying the firm's triangular metal logo.

A particular favourite, her fur-trimmed parka coats and jackets are perennially popular, combining luxury and utility, the 2006 ensemble designed to be worn with tortoiseshell-look platforms. Sarah Mower remembers, 'I chose Miuccia Prada's collection for Autumn/Winter 2006 because her show generated such a frisson of tension that seemed to connect with the unease at the time. The models looked almost like students striding to a neo-feminist political meeting – some of them were carrying books, a rare sight in fashion, and the atmosphere was compounded by an early '80s urban soundtrack, Grandmaster Flash rapping, "Don't push me, 'cos I'm close to the edge".' (Fashion Museum press release.)

In a tightly coherent and distinctive collection, Prada's palette was khaki green and grey, the shapes loosely based on military coats, large blouson-style tops with drawstring fastenings and calf-length evening dresses in silk. At the show, Sarah Mower commented, 'There was no mistaking the new attitude that was unleashed at Prada for fall. It charged out of the gate, looking young, angry, sexy, and serious – and dressed to tackle real life.' "I'm tired of being so sweet," declared Miuccia Prada. "We women should go back to strength – and the sober side. Stop trying to appeal to everyone, and go out into the world."

Adding the diffusion ready-to-wear line Miu Miu to the group in 1992, she continues to successfully design clothes which are enormously influential by nature of their versatility and practicality, whilst her luxury range of bags and luggage maintain a direct link to her first design for the company in 1979: a simple black nylon back-pack.

# 2007

## Giles Deacon for Giles

Orange 'Troubadour' dress with accompanying gigantic knit scarf, black and green feather-decorated sandals by Gina

Chosen by Hywel Davies, fashion journalist

Since 2004, the year he launched his first collection for his Giles label at London Fashion Week, Giles Deacon's distinctive sense of fun has meant plaudits from all sections of the fashion world, including British Fashion Designer of the Year 2006.

With a Paris training behind him, together with a brief stint at Gucci, Deacon has designed for firms as disparate as couture house Ungaro and high street volume retailer New Look, adding a fresh and distinctively light-hearted touch to both.

His orange satin 'troubadour' dress from Autumn/Winter 2007 is one of the most distinctive pieces from the collection, a demure satin cocktail dress accessorised with a huge chunky knit scarf. Following the theme running through the rest of the show, tightly tailored satin dresses were teamed with a further range of jumbo-knits, scarves and tops in tones of grey, burnt orange and green. His tailoring, beautifully draped, angular and sophisticated, added a distinctly haute couture look to a ready-to-wear catwalk. Mirroring the gigantic knits, his full-length evening dresses were accessorised with giant wraps of black feathers, the designer clearly relishing the drama created when experimenting with scale. Commenting on the collection he said, 'We just add and add and go mad, and we got on a real roll this time'.

His work on the High Street with the retailer New Look has ironically meant a whole new audience that might not necessarily follow his catwalk shows. With over ten collections for the retailer, 'Gold by Giles' launched in 2007 and became an immediate success. His clothes, advertised by Drew Barrymore and Agyness Deyn, were and are short, fun and affordable – dramatic, show-stopping party dresses in bold asymmetrical cuts and bright prints, slouchy tops and clever coordinates. As a couture and ready-to-wear designer he has had no qualms working for a high street retailer: 'I chose New Look as the high street store to work with, as we both have a sense of fun and believe in fashion for everyone'. (Fashion Museum press release.)

'The Giles dress was a beacon for edgy and contemporary fashion in 2007. The whole look encapsulated Giles's directional use of layering and experimentation with silhouette and proportion. The over-sized knit wrap was also highly influential and fuelled a medley of copy-cat incarnations.'

Hywel Davies

# 2008

## Karl Lagerfeld for Chanel/ Kate Moss for Topshop

Gold star and navy blue gauze trouser ensemble by Karl Lagerfeld. Long sleeve black dress with heart print motif by Kate Moss for Topshop

**Chosen by Paula Reed at** *Grazia*

For 2008, two outfits linked by one woman: Kate Moss.

Worn for her thirtieth birthday party, this was a vision from Karl Lagerfeld's Spring/Summer 2008 ready-to-wear collection for Chanel, with layers of tiny polka dots on midnight-blue chiffon, worn over star-print crêpe wide-legged trousers. Soft and feminine, vaguely 1930s in inspiration, it was an effortlessly glamorous creation seen on the most notable model of her generation, the ensemble a fusion of two talents for mutual promotion.

Paula Reed commented: 'Karl Lagerfeld at Chanel sums up the spirit of an extraordinary age. He embodies for me the Darwinian theory "it is not the strongest species that survives ... but the one most responsive to change". This ability to be ahead of the curve has distinguished Karl Lagerfeld's entire career. Chanel has achieved enviable strength in a tough market precisely because it embraces change so fearlessly.'

For those looking to emulate the model's very distinctive personal style, salvation came in 2007 when she designed her collection for Topshop in the first of a series of collaborations with owner Sir Philip Green. In a tightly coherent collection of stylish clothes – feminine, modern, quirky, many inspired by vintage shapes – she joined an increasing number of celebrity collaborators on the high street. Paula Reed agreed that more affordable does not necessarily mean less attractive: 'Great style is not about a bottomless budget – a high street dress can own its style credential as convincingly as a couture one. For me, the person who embodies the attitude better than anyone is Kate Moss. With access to every designer collection, a body to wear what she wants, and a lifestyle that gives her plenty of opportunities to wear it, the

woman spins her influential look from a combination of vintage, second-hand and designer pieces. She follows her own rules. Her guiding influence is what is right for her. She reflects the spirit of true style. And when she decided to produce her own collection it was not for a French or Italian catwalk. It was for Topshop, a British high street brand.'

Kate Moss wears Karl Lagerfeld for her thirtieth birthday celebrations, complete with gold star eye make-up.
*Daily Mail*

'We are living in extraordinary times. 2008 is likely to be seen by our children as a watershed moment; the end of a glittering party, when we consumed, celebrated and indulged ourselves like we were guests at a table groaning with good things that would never end.'

Paula Reed

Kate Moss launches her instantly successful collection for Topshop in 2007, appearing amongst the mannequins in the window of the Oxford Circus store.
Getty Images

'When I tried this dress on, I was amazed by the construction and the uniqueness of it. It was at once elegant and sexy and very very much its own dress.'

Gwyneth Paltrow

## Antonio Berardi

Black and white lace *trompe l'oeil* corset dress

Chosen by Lucy Yeomans at *Harper's Bazaar*

For 2008, two outfits linked by one woman: Kate Moss. Born in the UK to Sicilian parents, Antonio Berardi's debut catwalk show at London Fashion Week in 1994/5 came just as *Newsweek* magazine coined the phrase 'Cool Britannia', when a synthesis of music and fashion once again turned the world's attention to London.

Like so many successful designers, Berardi studied at Central Saint Martins and, after a period as assistant to John Galliano, sold his graduation collection to the department store Liberty, which had re-established its reputation for selling cutting-edge designers' capsule collections.

Alongside Alexander McQueen and Hussein Chalayan, he tempted fashion commentators back to London, where young designers' shows became ever more theatrical. In the process he established an international following. From the start Berardi's shows were the hot ticket for the international press and fashion buyers; even his debut catwalk presentation featured Kylie Minogue modelling a provocative lingerie-inspired dress.

Returning to London in 2009 after a period showing in Milan, his Spring/Summer collection met with widespread acclaim, his trademark style mixing sensual figure-hugging dresses in strong, simple shapes with accomplished tailoring. The simple black and white lace dress, corseted and tailored as an exercise in *trompe l'oeil*, hints at nudity beneath but, in fact, subtly conceals. Combining a graphic monochromatic look with a body-conscious silhouette, Antonio Berardi can claim authorship to two of the strongest trends of 2009. 'I tend to do what I know best,' he commented. 'Hard-tailoring, body-conscious and highly decorated, with a traditional twist.' (British Fashion Council/London Fashion Week website.)

Not surprisingly, his dresses have become a favourite on the red carpet for their scene-stealing qualities, and his faithful clientele includes Victoria Beckham, who commented: 'Antonio knows how to make a woman feel sexy yet still contemporary' (*The Guardian*, 28 April 2011). Gwyneth Paltrow wore the Dress of the Year to the première of her film *Two Lovers* in Paris in November 2008, providing publicity which saw pared-down copies appear on high streets across the UK within weeks. They achieved varying degrees of success, but none managed to match the original.

Gwyneth Paltrow continues to be a fan of the subtly revealing designs of Antonio Berardi, his white cocktail dress with black lace panels of 2008 worn by the star to the Paris première of *Two Lovers*.
Getty Images

'For me it represents the junction in her design oeuvre: the revolutionary ripped hems that she was the first to create 35 years ago in her punk clothing at her shop, Sex, and her study of the ladylike design codes of the British royal family that started in 1985. This dress is striking for its beauty and individuality, but above all it's the essence of the creativity of Dame Vivienne Westwood.'

Stephen Jones

# Dame Vivienne Westwood

**Evening dress in pale olive-green ribbed shot silk**

### Chosen by Stephen Jones

Vivienne Westwood is arguably the contemporary fashion world's greatest chameleon, having forged a stellar career which started with notoriety and rebellion and now thrives on her subtle reworking of an art-historical, establishment style. What began in 1971, with a series of counter-culture punk and New Romantic boutiques on London's King's Road, has grown into an international business, with multiple diffusion ranges and an instantly recognisable fashion signature.

For over thirty years she has drawn inspiration from hugely disparate sources. 'Pirates' began her catwalk shows in 1981 – a look which was memorably adapted in her styling of Adam and the Ants. Then, in a reaction to what she perceived as the aggressive masculinisation of fashion in the 1980s, the 'Mini Crini' collection of 1985 offered a fantasy confection of corsets, taffeta and ribbons as an alternative to the power suit.

Her 2010 shot silk evening dress from the Autumn/ Winter collection draws on a love of reinventing traditional couture. This is an area she frequently revisits – most notably in the definitive Watteau-inspired dresses of the 'Portrait' collection for Spring/ Summer 1996. In 2010, shimmering taffeta is again used, but in this case it is transformed into a longer hourglass shape, with waspish waist and elegant drapery; a homage to Dior's post-war New Look, but skilfully deconstructed and injected with both sex appeal and nostalgia. The opulent, structured bodice reminds the wearer of Westwood's skill in honing luxury fabrics, whilst the unfinished edges of the skirt hint at the recurring theme of subversion, preventing the design from becoming a mere facsimile. The style is part Grace Kelly, part rock chick, as Westwood understands what today's fashion stars want.

She is as famous and instantly recognisable as her clothes, and her many celebrity clients covet her ability to accentuate curves to the limit, producing designs which are at their very best on the red carpet. Westwood's influence is widespread, and indeed widely copied, as her ability to combine the risqué with an astute commercial flair means she is rarely out of the spotlight.

Chris Moore/Catwalking

# 2011

# Sarah Burton for Alexander McQueen

**Evening dress in ivory tulle embroidered with feathers and silver bullion eagle motifs**

**Chosen by Hamish Bowles, US *Vogue***

As head designer at Alexander McQueen, Sarah Burton has proved beyond doubt that she shares both his distinctive artistic vision and his ability to create exquisite couture clothing. Her training was based on a natural talent, first at Manchester Polytechnic and then during an internship with the company following study at Central Saint Martins. By 1997 she was Lee McQueen's personal assistant, later becoming head of womenswear, presenting her first collection for the label in 2010, the same year as his untimely death.

Her Autumn/Winter 2011 collection for Alexander McQueen remains her masterstroke, with Alexandra Shulman for British *Vogue* commenting, 'I thought it was amazing and as if the McQueen woman had been unshackled somehow; she was freer than before'. It was a feeling shared by other commentators at the collection, who noted that many of the darker elements of the traditional Alexander McQueen couture spectaculars had been subdued, reflecting a new sobriety in the label's history. This is mirrored in the 2012 Dress of the Year, which combines traditional and highly specialised embroidery techniques with bold symmetrical cutting to the skirts. Like John Galliano and Vivienne Westwood, Sarah Burton flirts with history, but her look is uniquely and firmly her own.

By the beginning of 2011, her notable success in establishing her own fashion signature and the dramatic all-white Autumn/Winter Collection inevitably placed her on the narrowing list of possible designers of Kate Middleton's wedding dress. In the event, she produced what very few commentators thought was possible: a design that combined the elegance of tradition with contemporary and innovative touches, most notably in a complex and layered peplum and train.

With the backing of parent company Gucci, Sarah Burton's success is enhanced by the fact that she now produces daywear with the same ease. With the patronage of the Duchess of Cambridge, she looks set to continue her glittering career as one of Britain's most commercially and artistically successful designers.

Opposite page
Photograph by Kirstin Sinclair. Taken from
*A Front Row Seat*, ACC Editions, 2011.

'Nowhere are Sarah Burton's unique skills better exemplified than in this magnificent dress that dazzlingly updates the tradition of the *robe de bal*, looking back to the crinolined Second Empire creations of Charles Frederick Worth and the mid-century masterworks of Christian Dior, but with a cut, technical treatments, and embellishments that are uniquely twenty-first century.'

Hamish Bowles, US *Vogue*

# 2012

# Raf Simons for Christian Dior

**Embroidered and appliquéd cut-off evening dress worn with black pencil trousers**

Chosen by Vanessa Friedman at the *Financial Times*

After the tumultuous years of John Galliano, any designer appointed his successor at the house of Dior faced a daunting task. Galliano's approach, until his unexpected departure in 2011, had been to accentuate the traditional role of the couture show, ensuring continuing success for his diffusion lines by provoking coverage in the press with a mix of high jinks and exquisitely created, exotic, theatrical collections.

The task, and perhaps one of the most coveted jobs in fashion, fell to Belgian designer Raf Simons in April 2012. His debut collection, warmly received by the fashion press, executed a masterstroke by comprehensively referencing Dior's New Look of the late 1940s and early 1950s, but firmly updating it for the 21st century.

Using a corseted bustier style that literally provided the foundation for Dior's post-war work, Simons' finely embroidered, beaded and appliquéd floral silk is as delicate as the finest ball gown produced in the golden years of the 1950s. With the dress cut short, to hip level, and combined with black pencil trousers, the ensemble could only belong to the 21st century, the designer successfully stamping his own signature on his tenure.

Vanessa Friedman commented: 'This dress, or rather [this] evolution of the dress, from Raf Simons' first couture show for Christian Dior, represents not just a generational shift in fashion – the moment when a new designer took over at the ultimate French couture house – but also an aesthetic new direction.'

Another favourite, and one which appeared throughout Simons' 2012 collection, was a version of Dior's 'Bar' jacket, featuring the structured, nipped-in waist and accentuated hips that helped to establish the reputation of the house in the late 1940s. Again, Simons teamed his version with the elegance of simple pencil trousers. In a series of further nods to the label's heritage, he showed razor-sharp, tailored, calf-length cocktail gowns with huge circle skirts, lean and figure-hugging 'wiggle' dresses, and grand floor-length ball gowns – all uniquely his own, but all with the definitive look of Dior.

# Afterword

Sugar pink silk organza lace and gem dress with black gaffer tape, worn with striped stiletto sandals by Sophia Webster and canvas cartoon character cap by Nasir Mazhar

Dress of the Year 2013
Chosen by Susanna Lau aka Susie Bubble
www.stylebubble.co.uk

Providing more signposts on the fashion map, for the Dress of the Year 2013 the Fashion Museum acknowledged the increasing importance of the internet and social media to the fashion industry and asked accomplished blogger Susanna Lau to select the award. Her choice of Christopher Kane's diamante and lace-embellished dress from his Spring/Summer 2013 collection focused on one of the strongest recent fashion trends with a nod to vintage couture, in this case the slender cocktail dresses of the late 1940s, but with the contemporary and challenging addition of gaffer tape.

Like the punk movement sticking a safety pin through a portrait of the Queen, Kane's demure ensemble is a defaced beauty, focusing on the deconstruction of luxury, with both Raf Simons' 2012 take on Dior's 'New Look' and Vivienne Westwood's love affair with reinventing the grandest couture exploring similar themes. Lau's choice of accessories in pink and black 'Liquorice Allsorts' striped stilletto heels by Sophia Webster and a pink canvas cap by Nasir Mazhar also recall a previous Dress of the Year award – Karl Lagerfeld's 1991 deformalistaion of the classic Chanel suit with denim, baseball cap and trainers.

As the Dress of the Year Award enters its sixth decade, the changes in the fashion world since the first award have been immense, but surprisingly there are many things that endure. When Mary Quant designed her simple shift dress in 1963 her aim was to free the young from the need to dress like their parents but, contrary to many predictions, haute couture still remains the primary influence on what the majority of people eventually wear. Just as in the 1960s, what is shown on the catwalks of London, Paris and New York is adapted, diluted and copied before ending up on the British High Street. However, with many designers now half the age of their predecessors, a sea-change in the most successful fashion houses acknowledges the need to appeal to a wide clientele – at one end are the stars in 'red carpet' dresses attracting press coverage; at the other are perfumes, accessories and make-up.

It is heartening that, as a direct result of the Dress of the Year awards, a permanent and accessible record of the twists and turns of fashion is preserved for those who wish to see it, allowing them to be the ultimate judges of each outfit's place in fashion history.

# Index

**Acknowledgements**
With thanks to Colin McDowell and Iain R Webb;
Rosemary Harden and all at the Fashion Museum,
Bath; Robert Shaw at Northbank; Liz Eggleston; to
the many designers and journalists involved in
Dress of the Year for access to their archives;
Matthew Freedman, James Smith, Anna Morton
and all at the Antique Collectors' Club; Peter Stone,
Dan Brown, Maggie Holt, and as ever to Geoff Cox.